VESTAVIA HILLS LIBRARY
VESTAVIA HILLS   ALABAMA

LOITERING WITH INTENT

Peter O'Toole

LOITERING
WITH INTENT

THE CHILD

HYPERION

NEW YORK

B
b'To P
c. 1
v. 1

Library of Congress Cataloging-in-Publication Data
O'Toole, Peter
Loitering with intent / Peter O'Toole. — 1st ed.
p.   cm.
Contents: [1] The early years
ISBN 1-56282-823-1
1. O'Toole, Peter.   2. Actors—Great Britain—Biography.
I. Title.
PN2598.O7A2   1992
792'.092—dc20
[B]   92-43478
CIP

FIRST EDITION
10 9 8 7 6 5 4 3 2 1

To Patrick

WE SHALL leave this old house and move elsewhere. So, come with me now to ramble up and down these steep familiar stairs, to wander and to muse in and out of all the rooms, to truffle and to shuffle through the drawers and the cupboards, to give a glower or a gaze at the pictures on the wall. What's this? From an aching old filing cabinet in my study I've plucked out a document. A formal and a formidable chunk of paper it is too, all embossed with an eagle and a crooked cross. It's a typewritten list of the names of nine lieutenant colonels, confirming their promotion up to perhaps model major generals, and signed A. Hitler. A for Adolf. A sight of that signature and my water swills uneasily. It's a practically vertical foul little gash. The document was given to me as a present by a brilliant, devotedly potty South American chum who both collects and distributes such fine things. My first sight of Hitler's inky monniker surprised and disturbed me. Looking at it now disquiets me still. Once, when peering through a book on graphology, I chanced upon a copy of the thing. Under it was the author's interpretation and category: Depressive. Well, yes, that too. We met in a cinema, Hitler and I, and who knows now that once there were in England two noble institutions, the news cinema, with its hour-long programme and the Moo Cow milk bar?

Up on my old Pop's shoulders when my age was five or so and the world was young. My legs about his neck and dangling down his nattily suited chest, my ankles in his fists, my hands gripping the rim of his billycock bowler hat, and we stalked on. At times, for the crack and for the ritual it prompted, I would shove the hat down over his eyes. His tall frame would wave about pretending to unhorse me, tumbling past the ever-present fag in his gob, chuckling threats reminding me that although he was temporarily blind he

I

was still not deaf and that was the clang of a square-wheeled tram he could hear approaching rapidly, and my time had come to be tossed into its mangling clatter. Oh, no, Daddy! Of course, I would relent, would tug up the hat from over his eyes, would, indeed, tug up the hat from off his head, would plonk it on my own and, for purchase, would grab his ears. Further mayhem would be on offer: erect and savagely he would gallop through that open doorway leaving me firmly imprinted on its lintel, he would disown me as a sack of spuds, he would do such things, what they were he knew not, but he would certainly sell me for sixpence.

Skittering and lurching along the pavement, at times just easily plodding along, myself aloft and my father safely supporting me, we stalked on. 'Malachi Stilt Jack am I, whatever I learned has run wild.'

Bliss was it in those days to be a child eight feet high in the air, happily with his Daddy, and, as was our gorgeous custom, heading for the Moo Cow milk bar. To scramble down Daddy. To hop onto the round leather revolving top of the stool. To hold in both hands the huge, cold glass filled and chugging with flavoured milk. To plunge the thick straw through the cool bubbles. To suck it all slowly and sweetly and deeply down, right to the squelching noises at the bottom of the glass. It was a demi-paradise of mine, the Moo Cow milk bar. Pop called it my pub. His pub would be round a cobbled corner. His flavour was whiskey from the wood and a pint of plain.

On those spiffing days, though, he would manfully sink his pint of cow-juice, pronounce it good, wipe his and my lips with a linen hanky and, so refreshed, would pay and then pass on, holding my hand now, purposeful, concentrated, and making with all convenient speed for the splendid news cinema. Modestly sized and a comfortable little spot was my long ago, well-remembered news cinema. Near to the front as could be, Daddy and I would plushily park our bottoms. Chocolate would be eagerly chewed, chatter would be eagerly heard or joined, but presently all the jaws would still and darkness would quietly enter the small auditorium ushering all our eyes towards the colourfully lighted curtained screen, and then the curtains would part. Music bombasted mightily out, a huge cockerel ecstatically crowed, a grand camera spun whirlingly around, time marched to drums and trumpets, Chinese junks sailed into blood-red sunsets, skippered perhaps by the great and good Popeye, champagne bottles swung to smash and froth on the sterns of huge ships as the ships, in turn, majestically glided down their chutes and plunged into the rude, foaming sea.

Will the elephant with the blaring trunk, the winged ears, the looming tusks and the immense feet come thundering out of the splintering screen, pursued maybe by the Ritz brothers? Will Donald Duck be on today? Or a king or a cricketer, or a boxing match or the Three Stooges, or a hurricane or a Zulu? Who's this? A uniformed fat man with a big chin, all wobble and posture and rant. The audience is booing him. It's Mussolini and he's being booed; cheerfully and vulgarly and ripely booed; but booed in the way that you'd boo the Demon King in a pantomime. Comical villainy to be encouraged with a raspberry jeer.

Shortly after, in that cinema, Hitler and I met for the first time. It is impossible to tell you what I felt because, other than being temporarily unhappy, I cannot remember what I felt. When that profoundly strange, mincing little dude from Linz came all unexpectedly onto my screen, not his hideous mouth nor his noise nor his moustache nor his forelock, swastika, salute, eyes or frenzy disturbed my mind; it was the look on his face. He was booed too. The audience boos, though, were of another colour; a grimmer lowing, an ugly note not for pantomime villains capering about banana skins, though there was to the concatenation merry laughter and choked damnations of the man.

There exists a photograph of Hitler taken almost exactly eighteen years before my birth. War had just been declared between Germany and Great Britain. He is seen quite clearly standing among others on a sidewalk in the Odeon-Platz in Munich and he seems transported. He could be staring at a brass band or an apocalypse but that's not it; it is the look on his face.

Years later, while diligently pretending to be a novice photographer and journalist on a provincial newspaper, I was reading a book on Hitler and in it was that photograph. In time relief and unquiet resolved into chords of confirmation in me. Yes. This was the man who had disordered a demi-paradise of mine twelve years ago. Hitler and I had met again, this time in a book. You see, in 1938 and 1939 when I was five and then six, all angels looked like Harpo Marx, all great statesmen used a cigarette holder and were Franklin D. Roosevelt, legendary sportsmen dressed in white, wore a tilted cap, flourished a bat and were known as Len Hutton, God had long whiskers and blew ships across the map; but evil was Adolf Hitler.

Throughout the terrible years of the 1939–45 war and the austere years of its aftermath, as I slowly grew up to be a man, my perception of Hitler, my picture of him, shifted ceaselessly as our English propaganda gave us him in crazed reflections of the truth it distorted. We learned of Schickelgruber, the former paper hanger and failed beer-hall putschist, of the Mad Muftie of the Long Knives, of the coward rat cornered in a bunker in Berlin committing suicide; later, and abominably, of the architect of Auschwitz. Countless photographs, newsreels, tales of all sorts featuring Hitler soaked into our senses. Lord Haw Haw pronounced from the wireless his idea of cultured English as he drawled to us his unfettered devotion to his Führer and broadcast the received truth of how the war was going the way of his Iron Warrior, Adolf Hitler. When William Joyce, in the person of Lord Haw Haw, lambasted some perceived pomposity he was a guinea a minute but mostly he was a bore. Hitler despised William Joyce, the scarfaced Connemara Yank and scholar with the demeanour of a streetfighter. A recording of one of his later broadcasts exists. It is 1944 in Hamburg. After the onslaught of the bombs what little is left of the city is in bits and burning. Joyce is in his recording

4

studio, pissed as a wheelbarrow, slurring out obscene grovel about what his great, world historical figure and leader, A. Hitler, could still do and what the man meant for the world. A lot of the world already knew that and we in England had had a hint of the plot.

Hitler's language passed my understanding but, I fancy, it went something like this. 'It's your chosen Redeemer, folk. Listen to me for a while till I tell you something, you who have come from farm and pit, mill or factory, breadline, dole, soup kitchens, home, office, school, hospital, prison, or Linz. More cake for Germans! Anybody's fucking cake. Because we are the best. More, my kindred own folk. I alone shall decide who is a German.' Joyce was executed in London after the war. Years later, in the late sixties when old central Dublin was being tumbled down, an Irish broadcaster friend decided to record the oral impressions that literature had made on some of the astonishingly well read plain working people of Dublin. He interviewed a flower-seller in the markets, call her Rose, and asked her what she thought of James Joyce. 'Oh, son,' she said, 'they were right to hang him!' Ah well. 'Jairmany calling. Jairmany calling.'

That photograph of Hitler, taken on the eve of the 1914–18 war, when he was twenty-six, practically destitute, anxious, fugitive, indolent and desperate, is worth a look. In a great bloody paradox it is likely that that war saved his nervous, frightened life, nurtured it, disciplined it, gave it personality, esteem, a legend and a voice. He was at the front for four years with the Bavarian Reserve Infantry, known as the List Regiment. Fighting for patches of mud the size of Hyde or Central Park, six million soldiers were killed. Infantryman Hitler's task was running messages from Command, across six or so thousand yards of heavily bombarded entrenchments, to the front line and back. The job carried a very high death risk. Officers of the segregated German military caste could not have helped but notice him; and he them. After their defeat they made him a V Man, a sort of education officer whose office was to explain to the dismayed and dislocated, conquered German soldiers, who had truly believed that they were only inches from victory, that they had been betrayed by politicians. The German High Command, itself responsible for the surrender, needed to be blameless. Hitler, they thought, though odd, was manipulable and had a strange gift of the gab.

The sight of that photograph eventually stilled my mind because I admire still the louche, noble courage of Franklin D. Roosevelt, the matchless resolution and flair of Sir Leonard Hutton, whether flogging 364 runs off Australia at Kennington Oval in 1938 in the shadow of the gasworks, or skippering his country when I was twenty-one, and winning the Ashes.

God still cracks his cheeks blowing ships across maps; Harpo Marx is still all my angels. Reassurance was at hand in that photograph; Hitler is evil.

———————

WHEN WE were six, Adolf and I, our fathers each followed by-ways to which they were not used.

Though he continued to wear it to church on Sunday, Hitler's Daddy technically handed in his old hat and his official Franz Josef fancy dress. At the age of fifty-seven he retired from a comparatively important post in His Imperial Majesty's Civil Service. He had been a senior customs man and had achieved extraordinary eminence for a man from an isolated Danubian upland, of a family of barely literate, agricultural labourers whose existence was harshly mean. Alois Hitler's education was minimal; at the age of thirteen he had begun an apprenticeship in Linz as a cobbler but, having served his time, he didn't cobble a lot. He became a customs man. He must have been very good at something for, in time, he became a District Chief Superintendent. When he walked by, most other customs men stood to attention. He was the cock of the walk. The embodiment of constituted authority which, commentators and photographs agree, was a role he fair ate.

He impressed his authority on quite a number of towns, too,

because in his last twenty odd years of customs service he had set up clink in ten different districts. Taking with him his wives and their children. Not that any of the places where he had lived were very far from each other. All roads led to Linz. However, at the age of fifty-seven, he gave the elbow to smugglers, thieves and swindlers and, with the missus and the kids, including, of course, six-year-old little Alf, he settled down to respectful retirement at a little spot near Linz; and kept bees.

When I was six my poor old Pop was a busted flush. 'On the floor', as he would put it, 'very Humpty Dumpty one'. His good fortune had taken a fierce tumble. A whimsical quarrelsomeness in his character may have cheered matters along but by 1938, as he was nearing his fifties, he was rapidly going skint. Boracic lint. Broke. Potless.

Of an Irish family, he had served an apprenticeship as a metal plater and shipwright in the North East of England where my Grandmother ran a pair of second-hand furniture shops. Daddy had not enthusiastically practised his trade, he had preferred a sporting life. In the twenties and thirties he had for a while flourished as Captain Pat O'Toole. His only known captaincy had been that of a minor professional soccer side. He had renounced all metal plating and had chosen to be Captain Pat, giving it leather all over the green goal-posted park.

At the end of the Great War his twenties were running out, as were his footballing legs and he turned to Lady Truelove, gambling. Captain Pat lived his thirties and early forties as an itinerant, racetrack bookmaker. Poker was known, as were chemmy shoes, spinning wheels, balls of all sorts, dicing, horse-racing. Yes, he would, when the bag was healthy, step off the stool, loan possession of it to his associate, Red Dan the tic-tac man, depart the Silver Ring and go punting in Tatts. Boxing matches featured, with wagers on their outcome, dice, dogs, point-to-points, which raindrop would be the first to slide down to a line fixed with breath and fingers at the bottom of the railway carriage window or, in hot temperatures,

7

to wonder for white fivers which cube of sugar would a fly settle on first, the left one or the right one? Even fiver the left. Bets off the draw.

From my birth up to my fifth year quite a lot of my exact whereabouts and those of my parents are difficult to follow. Some things are clear. We began to winter regularly in Leeds, in the north of England. For those who had blown it in the Smoke, that's London, either go North or turn it in was usually the trick and Leeds was known to the racing fraternity as the Golden City.

There was, it seems, in the soot-blackened Golden City, a tolerance towards the complexities of putting your money where your mouth was; a moderate climate for the horse players, the Sportsmen, The Fancy. In safety, they could step into the discreet gaming houses which waxed in a district known as Murder Mile. Jeff, in Keith Waterhouse's excellent play *Jeffrey Bernard is Unwell*, says of my father's, and throughout my childhood, my world, that it is 'stuffed with criminals, idiots, charmers, bastards and exceptionally nice people'. Daddy was all those bar one. He was only technically a criminal. Things fell off lorries, gaming laws were flouted and certain hard-faced men were either avoided or met and left blandly. Hypocritical, yes, in those times, but he was a decent and a gentle man who showed me fortitude, love and good humour. When the racetrack wars were being fought in the twenties, my old Pop wouldn't pay the contribution anticipated by an organisation for the protection of bookmakers. Pinky popped round to see him and hit him on the head with a coke-hammer. Think of that. Your ordinary hammer could kill, do you see, as could a filled bottle of booze. So to demonstrate what could happen to you if you were unprotected, Pinky had preferred as the instrument of his golden mean between murder and grievous bodily harm, either an empty bottle or a coke-hammer. A coke-hammer, Lord love you: you could give a man a great crack with one of those.

Violent, yes. Twice I saw him fight and once, quite unexpect-edly, we met in a pub immediately after he'd had a brawl. The fights were both times part of a general fracas. As he punched and kicked his share among the best of them, I saw that he was weeping. It was his custom, I learned. How different from many of us, I fancy, who would prefer to have the other fellow do the weeping. It was his wonky way. He was a contrary hoor.

My mother, Constance Jane, had led a troubled and a harsh life. Orphaned early, she had been reared in Scotland and shunted between relatives; but she was a joyful, very pretty girl indeed. Years later, a letter that we dug up when our friend McGilligan and I were scavenging for scraps concerning my parents, describes my mother at twenty as having wavy black hair, quick eyes and a determination to marry for money.

Things came fearfully unstuck for Constance Jane Eliot Ferguson when she bumped into Captain Patrick O'Toole.

In those times to picnic all along the ground close to the track was the thing. My mother, who was nursing at a hospital adjacent to this particular racecourse, one day thought that it would be a lark to have a day at the races with a picnic. Sitting on a rug enjoying herself in the company of chums, having a quiet chew and a sip, Mummy was approached by my father and from then on for Mummy, times were no longer a picnic.

Later, in her nurses' hostel, sitting alone among telegrams, desperate messages, dead flowers and telephone numbers of where he was or would be, perhaps she had mused on the events of that day and her encounter with Captain Pat. This, I fancy, is the way that it went.

'Good afternoon, nursecake, don't move an inch. Patrick O'Toole has hopped off his stool to be at your command. My advice is to keep your pennies prisoners but, should you or your friends fancy a bet, my clerk, Mr Archie Woodbine, advises me that Peasblossom will piss the next race. The going is good, the odds are eighteens, the jockey's bent, lay half a bar each way it will yield you sixes if he finishes in the frame, so can you muster eight half-crowns to back your splendid fancy?'

Mummy, it seems, had been deputed by her party to invest their carefully collected coins, the beast came in third, Daddy strolled back to them bearing their winnings of three pounds plus their stake and handed her seven crisp ten shilling notes.

Somehow and somewhere in the weeks and months following that day at the races, my father and mother came together and stayed together for close on fifty years, not all of which were without bumps. For reasons which have never been satisfactorily explained, minor adjustments were made to the official records of their lives and those of their kin. The family version of my date and place of birth is June, 1932, in Ireland; the same event is recorded as August of the same year at an accident hospital in England; my baptism was in November, 1932, also in England. There are slight but charming variations of nomenclature on all three occasions. McGilligan and I dredged up this, and much other matter, while sleuthing around these islands nosing for spoor. My nationality is Irish, my blood lines run to Ireland, England, Scotland and, alas, Wales; for Jesus sake forbear and cursed be he who moves my documents.

THE LANDS that lie Eastwards of Linz were where Hitler determined his own folk should go forth and selectively multiply; by 1938 his eyes were more and more hatefully flickering in that direction.

WE WERE living at that time in a little stone house on a hilly suburb of our Northern city, handy for the cricket and the rugby ground, and not far from my enchanted Roundelay Park. It seems that when I was four my father had chosen to quit this rambling life of his and, stating his occupation as 'traveller', decided to settle into a life of comparative peace and domesticity in our little stone house next to Mr Mole the milkman's dairy. Jangling with churns and jillpots, Mr Mole trotted out his horse and milk float of a morning, wheeling away to make his deliveries, while Mrs Mole and Mummy led me round on the donkey which was companion to the working nag and Daddy went into the betting-shop and card-shuffling business with Big Bluey and the Cockney Kid.

There may have been a little boy more happy than me, but if there was I should hope to see his photograph for the snap I have of me shows a grave, sweet child all golden-topped, easy, creamy as a cherub, gazing at the world with a deep, peaceful calm.

WHO WAS the villain who assured me that there was no Father Christmas? There was most certainly a Father Christmas. Didn't he come down the bloody chimney, knock back the tumbler of whiskey provided by my father, fill up our stockings with oranges, nuts, gobstoppers, a new penny and a sheriff's star, and then piss off back up the chimney again? To be sure he did. I'll fling that villain's lies back in his teeth! I shall creep down from my bedroom, past the sleeping loyal McGilligan, sit unseen at the bottom of the stairs and watch our munificent, white-whiskered visitor from the North Pole tumble onto the hearth-rug and go about his merry old business.

Now, in the days before the modern architect decided that we had no practical use for the street and Christmas trees were small and put up only on the actual eve of the event, the ways of towns and cities were often lined with various shops selling goods to customers and putting the purchases into brown paper bags. If you puckered the opening of the bag between an encircling thumb and finger, blew deeply into it, squeezed the pucker tightly and then gave the inflated paper bag a fair old smack with the flat of your free hand, it would explode with a delightfully loud report.

I am sitting in my pyjamas at the bottom of the stairs, inspecting the dark living room through the crack left after I'd opened the door just a touch. Someone is coming into the room, all right, but not down the chimney. The door from the passageway has opened, letting in some figures and a little light, but now the door has been shut again and all is dark once more. Bumpings about I can hear and my mother's voice chuckling and giggling. Daddy's voice I can hear now, praying aloud to Jesus Christ and then gurgling out quietly my mother's pet name, 'Connie,' he wheezes, 'Connie.' The light snaps suddenly on and there is Daddy, sitting on the floor, his bowler hat tilted over one eye, cradling in his arms a Christmas tree. Mummy is standing with one hand on the light switch, her legs are crossed, she is shaking and crying with silent laughter, her arms are through the handles of carrier bags, there are other bags on the carpet and brown paper bags strewn all the way to where Daddy sits. The determined little sight of me seems to quiet and surprise them a bit, as it quite rightly should. When I firmly ask of them if Father Christmas is coming, they are, at first, silent but very shortly Daddy begins praying again while Mummy now bends double making hooting noises.

Marching up to my father, I repeat: 'Is Father Christmas coming?' Daddy lays aside the Christmas tree, picks up a brown paper bag from the floor, unburdens it of its contents, slowly rises still holding the bag, walks in a curious way to the door, which he opens, and then exits the room, shutting the door behind him. There is a sort of silence for a second or two, a silence which is burst by a loud bang. The door opens and Daddy comes back into the room. He stands above me and looks solemnly down at me before pronouncing very clearly to me: 'Father Christmas has just shot himself.'

LIGHTNING FIRESTONE really did shoot himself. His eldest son had been killed in Spain, fighting for Franco. At the point of a gun he had locked his four remaining children in the basement, shot his wife to death and then turned the gun on himself. A picture of their children had appeared in the newspapers and was much talked of by the grown-ups. Whether or not his son's death had had any bearing on his wife's murder or his own suicide, no one seemed to know. They were dead, that was all. My mother was shocked, my father was silent, and both were very sad. An extraordinary man, Firestone, vivid in movement and speech, at times larky, at times aloof, brooding, at times, we now know, murderous. One time I asked my father why he was called Lightning. Daddy replied that when Mr Firestone turned up it was a racing certainty that shortly there would be a hell of a racket.

Did you ever see or hear of a racetrack bookies' clerk in the first half of our century? Accountancy on the hoof; rain or shine, on a hand-held ledger, drawn with a pen these rapid calculations in copperplate numerals and script. Lightning was one such. He had arrived in England from Australia with Big Bluey and other conscripted men, to fight for King and Country in the 1914–18 war, but had heard that in France they were using real bullets and so they'd immediately done a runner to the safer north where they kept their heads down till the guns stilled; and when the poppies bloomed they had put those heads together, formed the Australian Mob and thus team-handed had gone punting, dicing, gambling for a living, and they never saw the sun-dogs again.

Lightning was dead now and Big Bluey had avoided being so only by a whisker. Wearing his dark red, heavy silk dressing-gown with its black sash and fancy trimmings, he was hanging up a picture of his beloved Trudie, when the parrot on its perch suddenly gaped at the door and squawked alarmingly. Bluey had turned just as a gunman wearing a stocking over his head was loosing off a bullet at him. Bluey was already heading for the deck when the bullet got him. It went straight through the front shoulder of the dressing-gown, under the seam about an inch from the front left-hand lapel, came out of the back and wound up buried in the wall at the spot where the back of Bluey's tummy should have been.

Reinforcements had arrived, his assailant had scarpered, Bluey had copped only a nick which barely bled and which was nothing that a dab of iodine administered by Educated Evans couldn't fix. Bluey lived on for a good while, cherishing his parrot, his dressing-gown and his adored Trudie.

I was fond of Big Bluey, more fond of Trudie, but I couldn't bear the bloody parrot, I found it to be a thoroughly disagreeable brute. Trudie was a dote who, in her heyday, had been a high-kicking dancer and singer in the Edwardian theatre world. A photograph that she kept by her bedside shows her in a frock coat and wig, high heels and tights, kicking off at a charity football match, all dressed up in her costume as pantomime principal boy. Puzzling for some, our tradition of girls being boys and men being women as they are in our old ways of Christmas pantomime. Deliciously sexy, though, a man's doublet and hose when filled with the limbs and body of a fine woman. 'Breeches parts' these roles were called at the turn of the eighteenth century, exemplified by Fanny Jordan who bore to the future King of England, Sailor Bill, enough children to field a cricket team. Deeper, yet more playful still, the gorgeous sexual ambivalences Shakespeare so saltily, sweetly gives us with his Viola, say, or his Rosalind; girls played by boys playing women playing men, romantically confounding both women and men alike, telling us, the audience, to see what we will and to take it as we like it. Delightful, sublimely funny, moving glimpses of the frailties of our human condition.

***

HAVING FIRST dipped his heel into the faces of both friend and foe alike, the Führer Hitler had found that the flesh was good and yielding. So he had slipped on his jackboots and had stamped all over Austria at that time when Big Bluey had been shot. The Führer had, of course, popped into Linz. Such was the warmth of the welcome he had been given in his old home town that it seems he had decided on the spot to incorporate Austria into his Greater Germany, thus, as it were, keeping it in the family; something that the Hitlers of Spital or the Hüttlers of Strones or the Hiedlers of Döllersheim knew quite a lot about, and so did their sisters and their cousins and their aunts, their uncles and their brothers and their grans. Hitler's father had married his own cousin; indeed the poor cow who had given birth to Adolf may even have been her husband's niece. It may never be known precisely what their relationship was but Hitler's mother had always called his father uncle. Sensible commentators usually just print the Führer's family tree, leaving us to sort it out for ourselves. An awful lot of its branches are called Johann or Johanna or Maria Anna or Anna Maria. The Hitlers, Hiedlers or Hüttlers certainly had the consanguinity and were forever squabbling over wills, legacies, pensions and parcels of land. By false pretences Adolf had wangled for himself a very healthy orphans' pension, which, between the ages of eighteen and twenty-three, had kept him going for five of his years as bogus student in Vienna. He had then swopped the pension for a lump sum with an aunt or half-sister or blood relative of some sort and this had kept him with food and a roof until just before the eve of the 1914–18 war.

It is a vicious fact that although the Nazis insisted that millions of their subjects had to prove that their pure Aryan blood had been untainted for five or so generations, Hitler had been unable to trace back any further than his granny, Anna Schickelgruber. It has even been suggested that the Führer himself had Jewish blood; suggested but not proved. Whatever, only days after the Austrian *Anschluss*, Hitler had had the graveyard at Döllersheim, where his grandmother lay buried, transformed into a tank training ground and target range, eventually having the entire area covered with a thick crust of concrete, yards deep. That tit-bit came my way when I was seventeen or so. It chilled me then; it chills me still. More, on the eve of the Führer's triumphant return to Vienna, the city which had ridiculed and rejected him, TrueHenry

Himmler had been methodically peering through his *pince-nez* at a list of the 60,000 people who were that week to be arrested and slammed into concentration camps. While, perhaps even unknown to TrueHenry, a special unit of the Führer's personal secret police were scrabbling through files at the pertinent Austrian Ministry, searching for a dossier marked Hitler, A., which held the relevant facts of his abscondence from compulsory military service prior to the 1914–18 war. It would surely not do to have it known that the War Lord of the mighty and militant German nation had once been on the trot to dodge the draft, would it?

THE ATTEMPT by S. P. O'Toole, Esq., Traveller, to settle down as Turf Accountant and part-owner of a spieling joint, was not meeting with unqualified success. His reasons for trying this rooted life were obvious: stability for himself and family, hopes for prosperity, love of my mother and, of course, my education. In my sixth year I became a pupil at a modest Catholic boys' infants school, only a short distance from our house. It was fun.

My old Pop's preferred reading was either the newspapers or the *Racegoer's Annual Form and Handicap* book. My mother loved Dickens, Buchan, Galsworthy, Burns and could and did for our delight quote great chunks of Robert Service. 'Back of the bar at a solo game sat Dangerous Dan McGrew. And watching his luck was his light-o-love, the lady who's known as Lou.' My reading and writing, already nurtured at home by my mother, came on apace at school. Arithmetic and such proved a bugger but there were compensations: a concert we gave for grown-ups, I, as Professor Toe Toe, flourished a paper whip and fed sugar lumps to three other boys, one with cardboard ears, one with a string tail and one in the middle covered all with flour sacks, making up a six-legged horse. Serious crocodiles of small boys winding our way to awesome, hushed church for Benediction, a journey and service I loved. *'Agnus Dei qui tollis peccata mundi.'* The only time I can recall coming seriously unstuck was the day when I was drawing the horse pissing. It's a mighty sight for a child, a hairy great carthorse having a piss. The huge thick black truncheon of a penis, all veined and stretching, pouring out a waterfall of piss, streams of it shooting straight down onto the roadway, smashing and splattering there to suds and foam, making a steaming river running to the gutter. To describe this on paper during drawing was my intention. I was overlining with strong strokes of pencil the force and direction of the jet when Sister Aloysius peered over my shoulder. She gave a little squeal, she gave a little grunt, she summoned Sister Maria Concepta. Flapping, frantic as startled crows, rattling beads and crucifixes, black hooded heads, black winged sleeves, white celluloid breasts, hard, white bony hands banging, the brides of Christ got very cross indeed. They tore up my drawing and began to hit me. This made me more cross than those sexless bits of umbrella could ever be so I joined the dance and hit and tore. 'Tis only a gee-gee having a wee-wee you cruel, mad old ruins. Why are you tearing up my picture? Why are you hitting me? Have a footful of polished black shoe! And here are my milk teeth, round your earhole!'

Later, my little mother called on the school, probably wearing her posh voice with the long words attached. Someone must have taken notice for matters became less nasty, the fun returned. Still and all, though, there had been a change in the weather.

Then there was the business of my ambidexterity. An inherited facility for using my left hand when it suited. This was discouraged with whacks from a ruler. That was not to my liking at all. Not at all.

BRIGHT EYED little Alf went to school at Lambach where his father kept the bees. He was six. Sunnily disposed towards the world, it seems, he would toddle to the school holding hands with his sister, Angela Hitler. Very good at all his lessons, he sang in the choir at the beautiful church there, became an altar boy, romped with his playmates, was obedient and delighted in scampering all over his father's ten-acre spread. It didn't last. For reasons best known to himself, Hitler's Daddy chose to move the family nearer to Linz. Looking through copies of some of Hitler's surviving drawings, two only seemed to me to have any life: an ink, drawn when Hitler was eleven, showing a lacy swashbuckled figure, under whose large hat is a face wearing a spiked moustache. The face put me in mind of the face in a photograph of the 1914–18 soldier Adolf, only more cheerful. The other, drawn when Hitler was twenty-one, is a charming picture of his old school at Lambach.

WHEN MAKING a book or running the pasties, you only cop what others have blued. This is an immutable law. Others' losses make a bookie's winnings. Dynasties have been founded on the turn of a card. The trick is to own the premises on which the cards are dealt, to run, as it were, the book, to lay off bets, to cope efficiently with the vexed and shifting questions of legality, to provide dignity, decorum, safety and refreshments for your customers and, until the last race is over and the final hand has been played, never, but never, to dip into the takings for use in a game of chance yourself. Never. Running the firm is risk enough. Using the takings for stake money is not to be encouraged.

Daddy was blueing what he had copped. Moreover, certain principles of propriety were also in question. The firm's welfare was shaky, its health at hazard, and the Cockney Kid was getting up my father's nose. Little of this, if any, was percolating into our stone house. My mother had probably had a hint of the plot for very little went unnoticed by her. Mummy could spot the course, speed and given disposition of a passing fly; my little sister and I

were shielded from all harmful troubles. McGilligan was on hand
if needed and throughout our lives I saw my father raise a hand
in anger near the hearth only twice. One time was when I was
twelve, had been mitching from Sunday Mass and, answering an
enquiry from Daddy about my whereabouts during Mass time,
had lied in his face. He had suggested to me that I be a man and
tell him the truth and I had suggested to him that he was an old
bollocks who wouldn't know the truth if it bit him. I was hurtling
through the door trying to avoid the wrathful speed of him when
his hand caught up with me and gave me an unmerciful battering
about the bottom which left it fair humming for days. The other
time involved Cuthbert and the Cockney Kid. One day we had
a timid visitor; a mouse. My mother's tolerance and compassion
for humans was matched by her astonishing kindness to animals.
The jaunting days with Captain Pat had precluded ownership of
household pets. Dread of accidents between domestic animals and
infant children prevented us from owning them at that time. This
lack was remedied in after years when we were quite festooned with
all sorts of cats, dogs, rodents and budgies. Cuthbert's diffident,
velvet entrances and exits wholly enchanted me, my sister and
mother. Daddy, resting at home after the hard night-shift, found
our capers irresistible. As the days stretched on, Cuthbert, perhaps
sensing no harm, became less intimidated, bolder, more interested
in his whereabouts, curious, even, about my bare, tickled feet.
Daddy softly grumbled through his cigarette of the burden put on
the treasury by providing for a mouse. Mummy would regularly
burst into Burns. 'Wee sleekit cow'ring timorous beestie,' she would
intone, luring Cuthbert deeper into our household with fine edibles,
'What a panic's in thy breastie.' Our kitchen-cum-dining room was
at basement level at the front of the house and could be reached by
area steps which led down from the small garden there. Walking
down the steps one day, I could see through the window my mother
doing that strange business of crossing her legs, bending double and
softly howling. I belted down the steps, entered the room, Mummy

was still contorted and honking and my father was plodding about calling, 'Cuthbert. Come on, boy, grub's up,' and carrying a saucer of cheese.

Picture if you can the Cockney Kid discoursing on the state of the going at Ripon to my father, mother, sister and me as we sat around the room taking our ease, and seeing Cuthbert enter with unalarmed whiskers, making straight for a chewable at the base of the table leg. 'Pat, Pat, there's a bleeding mouse, see it? S'cuse the language, Connie, there's a blinking mouse, Pat, right there, see the bleeder?'

'Yes, kid,' said Daddy. 'We don't know what to do, it's eating us out of house and home.'

'Right,' said the Cockney Kid and in one movement he lifted his foot, smashed it down hard on Cuthbert, and crushed him to death.

There was a confusion of bodies and limbs across the room and out of the door. Through the window I saw the Cockney Kid's head snapping from side to side as Daddy pounded away at his face. He then kicked the Cockney Kid all the way up the stairs. Not since that day have I seen a man being kicked up a flight of stairs. Down, yes, but not up. Punched, grabbed, hurled and kicked, was the Cockney Kid that day, kicked, kicked, kicked all the way up the stairs; up and away from us as we sat there, shocked and grieving. It could not be long before the shutters went up on the old firm of S. P. O'Toole, Esq., Traveller, Big Bluey and the Cockney Kid.

Many years later, The Rook, a man who it was said had not been completely unaware of the arrangements made for the attempt to blow down Big Bluey, was killed in bed by his own son. Sonnie had crept through the garage into his father's house, planted a bomb, crept out, detonated the bomb and had blown the house, father and contents, to bits and perdition. He was nabbed within hours.

Bluey's Trudie died when I was sixteen. A malignancy had insisted that, one by one, both her lovely dancing legs be amputated.

Trudie had endured this with grace and good humour and her death was peaceful.

Five years later, as I was setting out to become a student at the Royal Academy of Dramatic Art, Bluey gave me fifty pounds, that was ten weeks' worth of money, a packet of a hundred Goldflake cigarettes and, yes, the famous dressing-gown, with its two neatly mended holes, for he knew I loved it and the story that went with it.

For a few months I swanked around my various London digs, peacocking about in it. I went to Ireland for a holiday and returned to find that our flat had been burgled. Most of my bits and pieces, my clothes and, of course, the splendid dressing-gown, had been stolen. What became of the parrot I just don't know.

———

ZEPPO SINGS simply a tuneful ditty to a pretty lady, telling her of a kid at the corner and the man in the moon saying I love you. Chico appears wearing a goblin's hat. The sturdy Chico sings too. He sings of how the cop and the burglar, too, say I love you. He sits at his piano wearing his goblin's hat. He plays. He sings. Confidentially, he leans towards us to tell us that everybody in the wide world say I love you. He plays his piano as no one else can or ever will be able to play. Strong, precise elves run in his fingers, to ripple them, to dance them, to flick, point, pick and rapidly run them up and down the keys. The firm inhabited fingers hop, tumble, skip and so accurately make their beautiful, tough and gentle music. See his face? Concentrated, calm, strong, mischievous, kind, telling us that he loves us, wearing his goblin's hat.

Harpo comes now. He fell from heaven in his topper and his raincoat. He can't speak, you see, but he has his honker in his belt and he paps it to tell us his thoughts. What's he doing now? Feeding a horse with flowers. He has found a harp, though, he always finds a harp. He will roll up the sleeves of his raincoat and will play the harp now. He's playing it! His great white hands spread and strum and cup and pluck and flow amazingly swiftly all over the strings. His thumbs run round in a blur of swoops and circles and God's music overwhelms and astounds us as his angel tells his message. 'I love you,' tells his messenger in the topper and the raincoat with the honker in his belt. His face is serene, powerful and lovely, his wide eyes closed to be peaceful as with joy he plays his harp.

A rubber duck is bobbling on the water of a lake. Pulled by string attached to the stern of a boat, we see. A fine woman is rowing the boat. Seated on cushions in the bow of the boat is Mr Groucho, strumming a guitar and singing to the oarswoman and the rubber duck of how every sucker and broad in the world says I love you.

The appalling, tormented end of King Kong upset me greatly. Gorgeous great monkey that he was. It was plain he meant no harm to the lady he held so carefully in his hand as he shimmied to the giddy top of the Empire State Building. You could see he was fond of the girl and only minding her. He wasn't going to squeeze her tummy or bruise or break her. Why hadn't they just let him be in his jungle? Wanting no more than to bump his chest, let rip the odd rumbling great yodel, chew a banana and fling a few trees about. Why capture him, rope and chain him, take him away to lock him up so that people could gawk at him? He was a superb beast. It was his capturers and keepers who were brutal. No wonder he broke loose and fled up the tallest thing to a tree he could find. But they chased him and found him and got him. They blinded him with searchlights, they wounded him with bullets, they set aeroplanes on him, to fly at him and frighten him and shoot, shoot, shoot him. Wicked they all were and cruel. It pleased me hugely when King Kong snatched the aeroplane attacking him and snapped it into bits. Serve it right. None of it was fair and may King Kong be blessed for ever for putting up a good scrap.

Mind you, there were hugs and sweets from Mummy to console. There was the sway and clatter of a tram ride to Roundelay Park to enjoy, ice cream to lick as my mother and I held sticky hands when we walked through the trees and down to my magical lake there.

Yes, I quite understood that King Kong was only a story, only a picture, it hadn't really happened. They were only pretending, they hadn't truly hurt that mighty monkey, it was just like a game. Mummy had explained it all simply and clearly to me as we dipped our hands into the water of the lake to remove the vanilla and the strawberry and my mother had thrown the last of her ice-cream cornet to the ducks. And yet: I didn't want to see that film ever again.

Things were altogether different with Arthur Askey and Stinker Murdoch who, you may not know, lived above Broadcasting House in a flat. Our wireless was shaped as an arch with the web of its speaker to match. This I took to be the window of Stinker and Arthur's home and had thought that they must be very small indeed to live in such a house. One night, possibly when big-hearted Arthur was singing 'I'd like to be a busy, busy bee, being just as busy as a bee can be', my curiosity as to how little Arthur could get in and out of the wireless prompted me to attempt a little breaking and entry at the rear of the set. Gently, my father dispossessed me of my jemmy, or poker or pencil or whatever I was using to effect this felonious entry into private premises. Daddy warned me of the mortal dangers that playing with electricity would surely bring; how Stinker and Arthur had the right to warble, chunter and chortle unmolested in their attic digs at Broadcasting House; that trespass or burglary would alert disapproval in both householder and Lily Law. I wanted to know if Arthur was very small. Daddy replied that he was, very. I wanted to know if Arthur was small as Cuthbert. Daddy said I was to think of Cuthbert on his hind legs, wearing a suit, spectacles and having no tail. Stinker? Daddy said Stinker was a bit taller, but only a bit. I wanted to know how Askey and Murdoch crept in and out of Broadcasting House. Daddy answered that it was a bit of a mystery all right, but that they probably entered and left when no one was looking, that to spy on or surprise them coming or going about their peaceful, cheerful business might startle them away from us and that would be a shame.

This was plainly sensible and so the peace of Arthur and Stinker was thus left undisturbed by me. Safe in their tenure of an apartment at the top of Broadcasting House, which was in our wireless, Big-hearted Arthur Askey and Stinker Murdoch were let be, regularly to entertain their listening playmates.

Eventually they must have moved to other lodgings where they assumed larger proportions, but this transition went unremarked, and troubled me not at all.

'Flying all around the wild hedgerows,
Stinging all the cows upon the parson's nose.
Buzz Buzz, honey bee, honey bee, honey bee.'

MY THREE-WHEELED bike was a wonder going down the hill. No pedalling, let them whiz, feet up, sit tight, zig and zag and ring the bell and steer these handlebars down and away, yes, ring the bell, mind the bumps, avoid the cart, and its horse, ring the bell, grip hard now and go wheeling right round this bend, that's it, mind the kerb, steer straight, grip hard, all's a blur and a bumping, bike shakes, eyes water, breeze is blowing, shuddering bike is slowing down, slower, slower, slowly now to stop at the bottom of the hill.

Push down on the pedals and turn into a quiet street. My legs are tired, though, my arms shaking from the juddering, my hands ache now. Off the bike. Bottom sore. Where am I? Giddy, puffed, and lost. Sit down on the pavement with my back against a wall.

My friend Thomas got only half-way down. He fell off. His nice dad told him off and sent him to bed. Thomas grazed his knees and

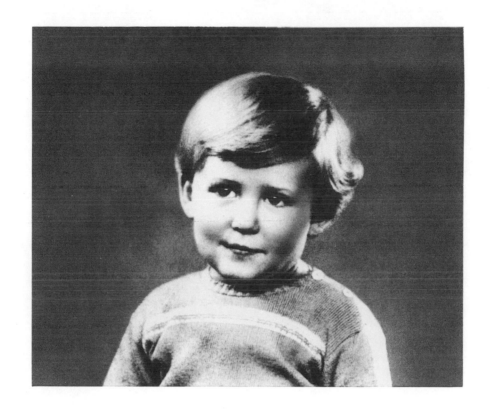

Peter O'Toole   1937.

?

hands. He will be pea-green when he hears that I went all the way and more. Feel better now. Puff coming back. Shaking still but it's a nice shake. Stand up. Wobble a bit but it's a nice wobble and I'm feeling lovely and tingly all over and very happy. Wander down the street a while, perhaps someone knows where I am. What's this? A cloth laid on the pavement underneath a lamp-post. On the cloth are pots and big paint-brushes. In one of the pots other brushes are dipped into what might be dirty water but with a burning smell. There is another smell all around the pots and the lamp-post, a deep smell, a smell I've smelled before. It is paint. Fresh paint. That's a smashing smell in the open air: fresh paint. And look! All the lamp-post down to where I stand has been painted with fresh, green, wet paint. Lovely. Feel. Sticky, thick, and bright green. From where my eyes are down to the bottom of the lamp-post has not been painted. It's all dry and scrapy and dark. Here is something for a lost tricyclist to do. He will help to paint with thick, wet paint the bottom bit of this here lamp-post, making all of it, from the top to the bottom, shine brightly with fresh green paint. The paint-pot tops are not jammed on, they easily lift off. The smell is gorgeous, the paint is very thick, the brush takes quite a lot of poking in, quite a lot of lifting out, quite a lot of spreading on the post, but my hands can help and do to spread this wet green paint thickly and fresh onto the dry scrapy dark bottom of this here lamp-post, helping to do the job of painting it a fine bright green. Brush and prod and scoop and smear and rub and smooth.

Tired now, hungry, a bit scared too, when my bottom, feet and the inside of my legs sometimes get stuck to the pavement and the post. The smell is not nice any more and all is sticky. To help to paint the lamp-post green is a hard job. My eyes smart, my mouth tastes nasty, I think I'm lonely and my tummy feels a little sick.

'Peter! Connie, he's here, Connie he's here. Look!' It's my lovely daddy. He picks me up and hugs and kisses me, getting himself all over green paint. He laughs until he cries and lets me wear his bowler hat. Mummy, now, giggling and hugging me and wrapping me in her cardigan and crying. I'm far too heavy to lift for long and so, having shown them my work, we three walk with me in the middle, all holding hands, around the corner, into a police station where, above white tiles, a big policeman laughs and laughs and, look, there in a corner is my tricycle.

The aftermath included stern dunkings in the tub before the fire, much dabbing with turpentine, some clothes seen to go whoosh up the chimney, and an avowal to my mother that never ever again would I wander away out of the sight of a grown-up, not never, ever.

Thomas thought I'd think he'd snitched on me but Daddy said that by telling the truth Thomas had shown himself to be a good, brave boy. Tom's dad agreed and, of course, so did I. Tom and I were then given an unmerciful bollocking by his father. Then my father put the block on us rightly by telling us that our tricycles were to be confiscated. We were grounded.

———

'THEY'RE OFF!' was the call to hurry to the finishing line and there, at the post or high above it, with or without binoculars, on or off my father's shoulders, to watch the horses and their riders as they hit the straight was my delight. The crowd takes up the race there. A low excited rumble sounds as the horses meet the two-furlong marker, the voices rise in pitch and volume and roll along towards you as the horses bound into sight. Colours flash, hoofs pound galloping towards you, whips flash, turf flies, and voices sing out riotous encouragement as the wild-eyed, foam-flecked horses hurl thunderously over the finishing line.

There is little time to listen to the voices of winning or losing punters who will tell you how their fancies had been nosed out at the death or had won hack cantering or had been beat a whisker or had won by a street, for there is the unsaddling enclosure to skip to. To see the graceful great beasts steam in to toppers and congratulatory pats.

The days always began walking from the car park to the Silver Ring. Young Tommy, who drove Daddy's black Citroën, Red Dan and Archie Woodbine would burden themselves with the stand, the stool and the brolly, book and bag. My father, mother and I would stroll through the gathering racegoers.

Tipsters would be in full cry, royally led by Prince Monolulu, feathered and leopard-skinned, tall and black, handing out his brown envelopes filled with sure things in exchange for cash. Escapologists to wonder at as they writhed out of their sacks, hoods and chains. Trick of the loop men, thimble-riggers and three-card sharpers deceived the eye with their quickness of hand. Tents held friendship and lemonade, chatter, beer, wise counsel, laughter and solemn assurances. The paddock let us see the big fine horses, brushed, sleek, blanketed and numbered, loping calmly around, led by their lads.

The jockeys would enter wearing their brilliant silks, to talk awhile, to listen, to point their whips, to be heaved up into the saddle by hands locked under their knees, to walk their horses around the ring, upon their toes some, others dourly plodding, some skittish, prancing, others calm and graceful, all beautiful. Then dash to the rails to see the horses stretch, leap and canter to the start, the capped, coloured jockeys rocking on their backs. A hubbub now of bookies shouting the odds, white-gloved tic-tac men semaphoring prices and vital information, bets taken and laid off, fancied selections, racing certainties, hot favourites and rank outsiders, short odds and long shots, all the ponderables of form, weight, course, distance, bloodlines and partnerships translated into cash wagers, nods and markers as the horses come under starters' orders. The punter puts his money on his fancy: and then they're off.

'LITTLE BOY kneels at the foot of the bed', Oh Lord love you it is my mother's spokensong version of Christopher Robin; it remains ineluctably plugged into my poor mind to this very day.

'Hush, hush, whisper who dares,
Christopher Robin is saying his prayers.'

Daddy kneels before the fire with a sugar bowl. There is paper, wood and coal there, a match has been put to it, the fire is lit, my father chucks handfuls of sugar onto it, they burst into lovely blue flames and go chuckling up the chimney. 'Expensive, Peter,' says my daddy, smiling and still wearing his hat. 'Expensive.'

Whose hand it is I do not know, nor when, nor where but still in front of me I see the large hand with the slice of crumbly yellow cake balanced on it. The hand seems lighted but all around is dim. Softly a voice speaks but I can hear no words, nor do I know if the speaker is man or woman. Another hand enters into the light, carefully plucks a chunk of yellow cake for itself, then goes up and out into the dimness. The hand is joined again by the other hand and carefully again and again until all the cake is gone.

What remains remarkable and memorable to me is that, from beginning to end, the hands did not spill one crumb.

'I GO THE way that Providence dictates,' said Dictator Hitler, 'with the assurance,' he added to chill, 'of a sleepwalker.' The nightmare somnambulist walked out one evening and broke all the Jewish windows for his Crystal Night.

'Kiss me, girls,' he said to his typing pool, 'I'm going to be the greatest German ever,' then, unopposed, he walked out one evening from the Sudetenland to Prague and in days Czechoslovakia was entirely conquered; and the black swastika flapped.

'Peace in our time,' said hopeful Neville Chamberlain, holding high his sheet of paper Adolf Hitler had signed that promised this peace.

The dictates of Providence had Hitler clearly murmuring that his opponents all were little worms and, abstractedly perhaps, thinking of Danzig and Poland, he took his sheet of paper that Neville Chamberlain had signed and wiped his fearful arse on it.

———

MY NOT going up the down escalator or down the up may have rumbled me but before our demure descent down the down escalator had ended, the tummy-ache, which had been giving me gyp all day, gave me a frightening twist of pain and my mother had me up in her arms when the escalator flattened into its grilles at the bottom. A taxi took my mother and me to a hospital. Acute appendicitis had caught me suddenly; the appendix burst leaving me with an infected abdomen, a peritonitis. This was before the days of the antibiotic, and the chances of a child surviving this ill condition were not good.

After an emergency operation to remove the source of the infection, I was stitched up and then a rapid move to an isolation hospital seemed to be the best hope for me. The ambulance took me to a hospital high on a steepy hill, above a proper Yorkshire village with its own steep, steep slopes and a petrifying witch.

> Dear Mumy and Dady
> I am very unhapy. They have taken away
> my Tedy and my magic set.
> X X X Peter

Complete isolation turned the trick nicely for me; and, no matter the groans of my letter above, penned to my parents when I was

29

six, it would have been plain to them by then that I was on the mend and beginning to spark once more.

Dim light, though, in this isolated room. Half light, night light, shapes and shadows; faces masked and covered, lighted by watchful eyes. Poultice, thermometer, ice pack, stethoscope put on me with rubber-gloved hands and here's a flat stick to poke in your gob and could you please say Aaagh? My mother, father and little sister pressed their faces to a window above the door on visiting days. There was comfort there and carefulness, human, kind and strong. Vigilance and skill, shown by both doctors and nurses, soothed and cooled my inflammations and my fevers and saw to it that I slowly recovered.

On release, my family was there. Their gratitude expressed to the staff and their happiness at being with me were exhilarating but months of illness, isolation and the laborious business of getting better had made a feeble little chap of me. I was also silent, distant and unable to walk very far. A car and then a train journey took us to a convalescent home on the North Sea coast. We parted there, my family and I. They visited me often and my days were never lonely. Fresh air, being seven, good grub and the simple society of others soon had me walking and talking and gradually building up a fair head of cheerfulness. Robin Hood was my favourite book then. Difficult at first to read, if the author's name was on it he will forgive me I have forgotten it, but the illustrations I see, one in particular. A dying Robin, grey and aged now, is sitting propped up on his bed, held there by Little John, his great oaken old Friend. Robin's bow is in his arms, bent, with an arrow set in it. He aims through the open window up over the lake, the river, and fires his final arrow into the greenwood to be his gravemarker.

A year or so before my tummy-ache we had been heading by car from a racetrack, aiming for the nearest boozer, boarding house, hotel, milk bar, news cinema, pitch and toss school, dog track, railway, card game, cricket match, or other gathering of frivolous fancy. We saw a sign for Kirklees Abbey, traditionally where Robin Hood secretly lies buried. Big Duggy the Zulu was with us. He was one of Daddy's betting playmates but he was my friend. He was very black, taller and broader than my father; he fancied white chicks something amazing and they him, a fact which fluttered not a feather of the tolerant racing world. He always wore or had with him a camel-hair coat. My feelings were that it was probably a bit more nippy here than it had been back home in Darkest Africa.

My mother was despatched with Young Tommy to buy lemonade and beer. Acting on inside information supplied by me, Daddy, Big Duggy, an appalled Archie Woodbine and I formed a foraging party seeking the unknown grave of the Green Man. Muddied, torn camel-hair coats, split wet grey spats, and bent bowler hats later, my enthusiasm for mud was contained. We all stopped floundering about in the nettles and the undergrowth, chopping with sticks at the lost, marshy bones of my hero. Knocking back our drinks and meat-paste sandwiches, Daddy mentioned that if Big Duggy had brought his *assegai* with him he could have heaved it from the spot where Robin had loosed his arrow and, pound for pound, Zulu and English outlaw, he reckoned that Duggy could achieve in three chucks what Robin had gained with one twang, thus giving us a notion of the true course and distance. Big Duggy said that it was a sporting idea, that if he were to use his best spear, which he kept in the bank, he would probably hit the spot in two and that he would remember to bring it the next time we were at Kirklees Abbey.

A few days later Duggy arranged to meet my father and me at a pub next to a Town Hall. It was a long summer's evening, and Duggy was standing on the pavement outside the pub as we arrived, carrying a large package. He unwrapped his parcel and gave me to keep a beautiful fully rigged three-masted model schooner. And that night, in the shadow of a Town Hall lion, we sailed my yacht in a horse trough.

Memories of other times, I fancy, that might have roamed

my mind after reading Robin Hood when I was seven and getting well.

————————

We had gone to war to fight Hitler, I soon learned, even as I was handed my gas mask. It was in a plain cardboard box which had a string strap for hanging on your shoulder. The contraption itself was strange. A little black pig with a window. A rubber article which was easy fun to put on but soon became a bugger to wear. Mine smelt of cold hot-water bottles and was difficult to breathe in, and the window misted up as I was trying to cop a squint of myself in a mirror. I took the whole of it off, hung it over my face and peeped at the reflected effect with one eye over its top. I saw a little black rubber pig. Leaving mine off, I went to look at the others wearing their masks. It was a strange sight. A tin-hatted gas mask wearing a uniform hove into view. Unmasked, it revealed an Air Raid Precaution man. He warned us of bombs and shells and poison gas.

Indeed, trenches were being dug everywhere, windows were coated with glued brown paper, air-raid shelters were being designated or built. There I learned what later, when I had returned to my parents, I came to believe. Hitler was a tyrant of insane bestiality who would, if let, torture and kill us all. We had to resist him and fight him, and in our war he would, with his Luftwaffe, pour down bombs and poison gas on our heads. Later yet, in a schoolyard somewhere, a group of us, grown-ups and children, all wearing gas masks, stood in a circle around a tin-hatted, uniformed little black rubber pig with a window that was handling a tear-gas canister. We were to test our gas masks. The canister was cracked open, thick white smoke poured out, I stuck my snout in and took a good whiff. Something vital may have perished in my gas mask or else there was a hole in it or it was on upside down but I sucked into my face, eyes, nose and throat a fair billow of tear gas. Like a dog I howled for hours, vomited, and my eyes burned and wept for days. My mother nursed me with boracic lint and eye lotion. Tear gas only: but we had heard of nerve gas, mustard gas and a gas that smelled of geraniums and was deadly.

HITLER HAD been poison gassed. Daring despatch runner he was, twice he was got. Shrapnel swept a bit of his shin away. After two years of carnage, fighting trench warfare at the front, he was got. Into beetroot fields, stream bottoms, slag heaps, pitheads, broken smoking juts of towns and villages, burned vanished woodlands, into downs and rides and hillsides, the trenches had been dug down deep into the mud and the earth. Duckboarded, sandbagged, cable and barbed-wired, these miles of gridiron slits gouged and mazed through Flanders and beyond. Hydra-headed, destroyed, constantly relocated, these barbarous earthworks moved and split the countrysides of France and Belgium. Six million soldiers hopped off sandbag parapets and were killed. Many miles of no man's lands ran between the Allied and the German trenchlines, they, too, dying and being reborn in other fields. Barbed-wire gardens to crouch in and be killed. The industrial revolution provided the First World War with a pippin. The metals and mechanisms of locomotives, sewing machines, and such, were translated into artillery and muskets. Guns could shoot missiles further, more rapidly, more accurately and in greater numbers than hitherto. Howitzer shells, coalboxes, aerial torpedoes, whizzbangs, trench mortar bombs, Jack Johnsons, seventy-sevens, eighteen-pounders, up to one-thousand-five-hundred-pounders the shells fell and burst on the enemies' positions for weeks at a time regularly for four years. Earth, rocks, chalk, barbed wire, trees, rifles, soldiers and sandbags spumed into the air to fall into flames and craters.

Fodder-fed, its maintained, oiled machinery efficiently ran the

Maxim gun and, portable and concealed, it shot six hundred bullets a minute into the mined, open killing zones. Nor did most soldiers see their intended victims: industrial techniques made that unnecessary. Often only the poor bloody infantry met their foeman face to face. And the poison gas, heavier than air, lingered round duckboard mud.

After two years of this our *Meldeganger* was got. He copped a Blighty wound, not fatal but incapacitating and ensuring a trundle back to the Fatherland for rest and mending.

Ten weeks after his volunteering for the Army, in 1914, Private Hitler had been sent to the front, at Ypres, Wipers to us, where he had arrived in time to witness the effects of the *Kindermord*, the Massacre of the Innocents, when many hundreds of untrained volunteer soldiers from German universities and high schools pitched themselves into battle and were entirely slaughtered. In a letter written at that time to his landlord, Popp the tailor, in Munich, Private Hitler tells of eighty per cent of his regiment dying in the first few days. At the age of twenty-six the deadly business of being a front-line messenger boy was to be the first regular job he had held in his life.

The one subject at which he excelled at his posh high school in Linz had been gymnastics, a skill which might have come in fierce handy when scuttling through trenches and no man's lands on the fields of Flanders as the immense tonnage of sparklers, plenty of it designated for communications trenches, paths and roads, came spluttering down around his feet. Nineteen fifteen found him still running leaping and tumbling at the battles of Tourcoing and Neuve Chapelle, sporting the Iron Cross awarded to him for bravery. In 1916 he was at the Somme, a battle that stays with us not only as a tragic military error, when a nation, protected by its navy for many centuries, realised that it could lose its entire young manhood by war, but also the Somme seems to be at the source of so much that our twentieth century poets tell us of war. As much as we ever will, we have studied all that war could do to men on the fields of modern battle when we read the story of the Somme. One million men had died, and Hitler was there. The *Meldeganger* was doing very nicely in his good job. Other than a couple of begrudgers, one who called him a white crow and another who said he was a grumbling know-all, he seems to have got on quite well with his fellows. Schmidt the painter and Meldeganger Buchmann were his mates and two other members of the List Regiment went on to become his disciples, Max Amann and Rudolf Hess. Sergeant Max, the clerk of the regiment, who in time became business manager of the Nazi publishing house and of Hitler's newspaper, the *Volkischer Beobachter*, or *My Own Folks' Gazette*. In the middle nineteen twenties, when they were both doing porridge, Fräulein Anna, as the Nazis nicknamed Hess, was midwife and typist to the birth of Adolf's masterpiece *Mein Kampf*.

In the autumn of the same year, 1916, he was got. The leg wound he copped at Bapaume had him tucked up snugly in Berlin for a couple of months, but by the beginning of 1917 he was back again trotting. Through the battle of Arras he trotted on. And the third battle of Ypres, at the trot. In the summer, for the second time, Lance Corporal Hitler was, again, decorated for bravery with an Iron Cross First Class, an honour usually given only to officers. These officers said of him that he was a disciplined soldier who had never let them down; it was a pity, they thought, that he lacked qualities of leadership, had no power of command, for he galloped like a good one with his messages and always wiped his feet when he came in. He wintered at the battle of Aisne. In the spring he went trotting in the thick of the last great German offensive, one which most Germans, population and forces, believed would lead to the final victory battles. Since the war had begun, Germany had been victorious in most of the major set battles. In what was to be their last triumph, in 1918, they managed to push our lines back almost to Paris. It was the last spasm of aggression, which exhausted the German army of men, ammunitions, supplies, food and endurance. The bitter end was near.

South of Ypres, in October 1918, we fired poison-gas shells at the enemy. Hitler was got on a hill. After four years of relentless trench warfare, the man who it was thought lucky to be near was finally down, gassed. Severely disabled he crawled to Command where, exhausted and temporarily blinded, he collapsed. Freighted to Pomerania, medical attention restored his sight but Lance Corporal Meldeganger Adolf Hitler Iron Cross First Class and Bar with Wounds, would *gang* his *melde* no more. Sitting up in bed, after two months of hospital, news of Germany's unconditional surrender to us found him.

Adolf was out of work once more and, very likely, soon to be once more back on the pancrack.

———————

JACK JACK the Levantine had tipped the wink. There was to be a reckoning. Rivals, disaffected colleagues, dissatisfied clients, moneylenders, stanchions of propriety, bonesplitters and blue Lily Law, geed up perhaps by the war and the evaporating wells of credit, were moving in on the more heterodox members of The Fancy. Bluey split, not to reappear until 1944. Big Duggy went too, and I never saw my Zulu friend again. Tommy, Dan and Archie went their ways to keep their heads down, surfacing from time to time throughout the war to bandy about whiskey, chocolate, cigarettes and chat.

Silky, the Flea and Justice Wrottesley moved in to Rowboat Annie's place north of the city. Bob the Liar, Educated Evans and the Wolf went to ground, others scarpered hither and yon, some went to war.

Daddy wrongfooted everybody.

In the late seventies, Jack Jack the Levantine and I sat and sipped, mused and remembered, marked and filled in each other's cards and blanks as we sat reminiscing in a pub where I was staying in the far Northern Dales. My father had been fond of the Levantine and Jack Jack of Daddy. The son of poor Jewish immigrants, he had been an illiterate, brilliantly resourceful guttersnipe and errand boy for a bookmaker. Encouraged into education and learning by the bookie, Jack Jack eventually became a lawyer. Respected and successful, he practised law for many years earning, among other things, a paragraph in a history of the capture and conviction of enemy agents. He knew a prosperous, interesting personal and professional life; he also remembered his more raffish chums from the racing world, provided them with counsel and help when needed, and he could be relied on to keep his mouth shut tight as an oyster.

He had been surprised to hear from me when I telephoned him at his office. Nearly eighty, he had been at his desk since six that morning. It was his habit. He preferred to have his pending paperwork done before partners and staff arrived. We agreed to lunch together at an hotel round the corner from his law firm. Walking into the restaurant, I spotted him. Small, spruce and dainty with lightful, bright brown eyes, he looked me over, listened carefully to me and then said, 'When you leaned towards me just now I saw your father's shoulders. You move like Pat but your voice is like Connie's. What can I do for you?'

When I had told that I was looking for light on people, places and events from time past that concerned my family and me, we agreed to meet again and indeed we did. We went to a spring meeting, did our pieces, fell into a pond of Old Peculier and wound up having a chew and a blather at my digs in the Dales. On matters that were public knowledge, however limited the public or the knowledge, he contributed to and even adorned some of the known facts. On matters that were not known to the public he said to me, 'Don't forget, Peter, the people that you and I are talking of, they knew that the best way to keep a secret was to keep it to themselves.' Right to the end, Jack Jack, mouth shut tight as an oyster.

───────────

CALL IT Hunsbeck. It exists no more; it has been demolished; it had been a slum. Bernard Shaw called it a black stain on the face of the British Empire. Built as homes for labourers in the middle nineteenth century these brick rabbit hutches had been studded up, squat and meagre, back to back, row upon row along criss-crossing cobblestoned miles of nasty, sunless narrow streets. Many had been gas lit, most had owned no bathrooms, kitchens or lavatories, few had had more than one cold water tap, all had had cramped small rooms, none had known privacy. These shelters and dormitories had been squashed between and around and up and down their places of work. Factories which had manufactured iron goods, steel goods, wooden goods, lead goods, rubber goods; engine-makers, string-makers, paper-makers, nail-makers; cotton mills, wool mills, saw mills; freight yards, gas works, coal mines, slag heaps, potteries, warehouses and tall, tall, thick, brick chimneys.

The whole district had been south of a noxious, fishless, dark yellow river and, to its east and west, there had been, for recreation, two open cinder-strewn spaces known as moors, while through the warrens and the workplaces had run railway lines, alleys, canals and cobbled, tram-tracked roads. Dotted here and there had been shops, pubs, pawnbrokers, a lunatic asylum, a few schools and churches, a dance hall, a billiard hall, the police and fire stations, the public wash-house, the picture houses, the public library and, in the shade of the pithead, the pride of the area, its gallant, fighting professional rugby club.

Everywhere, over everything and everybody, the lofty chimneys ceaselessly had poured out their vile slimy thick black soot.

Milky had made the arrangements. Milky had done bird. Bird lime; time; prison. His offence had been robbery with violence. He had also been sentenced to the cat; a flogging with a cat-o'-nine-tailed whip, a popular punishment in the first third of our century and still held in high esteem by some. For some reason Milky had been spared the cat but prior to his not getting it he had thought about it a lot. Apparently, this had given him severe trouble of the bottle. Bottle glass; arse, fear.

A tall withdrawn man, Milky. Tidily dressed, fleshy, bald, big-eared and jowled, dark, dull eyes, stealthy, quiet and punctual; he had always looked as though he'd just had a wash. But where did he come from, where did he go? No one seemed to know.

His brief had been to find us a spot in which we could safely winter. Somewhere unlikely; but handy. Away from the present fuss, but not too far away. Adjacent. It was to be for a short while only. True, times were hard, money was scarce, there were bitter ructions, but soon the flowers appear on the earth; the time of the singing of birds is come, and the voice of the starter is heard in our land.

'Find a dirty little spot and paint it.' This decision as to where our caravan would next rest had been reached by Milky and my old Pop only days before Hitler, with surprise, suddenness and frightfulness, had hurled his blitzkrieg into Poland, pounding and mauling that country into subjugation, and England declared war on Germany.

IT SEEMS that the Führer had very much hoped that England would not do any such thing, would indeed come to some sensible little arrangement with him, and that this determination to ignore his hopes and to oppose him sternly had given Adolf severe trouble of the bottle; his pucker being vigorously tested.

Prior to Hitler's invasion of Poland and our subsequent declaration of war, one of the lesser-known actors in the drama of those days strikes my fancy: Mr Dahlerus, Swedish businessman and honest, unofficial deal-broker between the German and the British authorities. At that time an aeroplane had been volleying back and forth between the two countries and Mr Dahlerus had been practically living on it. After landing he would enter either Downing Street or the Reich Chancellory, give and receive his instructions, exit, get on the aeroplane and then take off.

Mr Dahlerus is quiet about events at Downing Street, emphatically graphic about his scenes with the Führer.

Now; Dr Morrell the pox doctor had joined Hitler's firm in 1936. From that time on he had pumped the vegetarian, teetotal, non-smoking Alf quite stiff with drugs. Deadeners, liveners, barbiturates, cocaine; indeed all manner of chemical and herbal potions and nostrums were being shoved into the body of his living Führer.

Hitler had become and was to remain until his death, a drug addict.

It seems likely that the Pox Doctor Morrell had also sold his Führer the Mithridates system: small dollops of poison taken as an inoculation, to build up a natural resistance to poison. The Führer ate strychnine and belladonna with his nut cutlets.

Adolf's temperament had never been rock steady, he had always, when let, showed a rash facility for flouncing and tantrums. One may picture his state in those days and hours before the war; desperately longing for the English to come to terms, almost convincing himself that they would, knowing that if they didn't he would have to eat *Mein Kampf* and would have to face and fight both West and East.

When Mr Dahlerus turned up one night at the Reich Chancellory with Fat Hermann Goering it was past midnight and the Führer was deeply in snore. 'Gently wake the bastard up,' insisted Goering. 'Tell him it's Fat Hermann with Da Da the Swede. We bring starting prices, runners and riders and the state of the going at London.'

After orders to rouse Sleeping Hitler had been thus given, Da Da may have mused aloud, I fancy, 'There's not a lot to tell,

Fat Hermann, not a lot at all. The odds are the same, no one has scratched, and the going is thick as pigshit.'

'That's it,' said Hermann. 'Tell Golden Bollocks that. That will take the shine off his smile. He's been listening to some very shaky information from Kipper Ribbentrop. If he believes it then we are all fucked.'

It took a second or two before Alf showed up. It does, you know. If one has succumbed to a tap on the noggin from a pharmaceutical rubber hammer, arousal is not easy and often can only be sustained with a flake or two of some fine heartstarter. This may affect speech, movement and judgement. Picture then the now wide-awake, mad-eyed risen Alf. Fully dressed, moustache brushed, black hair flopping, lamp-lit white face haggard with perplexity and terror, stamping and lurching around the room favoured with his choice oil paintings, banks of orchids and exquisitely plush carpets.

See him pause his pacing, fix eternity with a stare, and hear the self-acknowledged greatest orator in Europe huskily slur and mutter to himself:

'Hear my voice my mightiest of own folk. Hear my right mighty voice as rightly you have mightily heard it for right mighty years. Might is right and right is might so it's all right my mighty own folk. We are us, you are me, I am us, we are me, it's miraculous, altogether, I am right irresistibly mighty. I, us, my, we, our military might might rightly smash, crash, bang, boom, wallop, clang, clatter, crunch, batter, bash, shoot, shell, shite, bomb, shite, shite, shite, rightily, mightfully, shitefully, all together now my own folk: "Germany over every fucking body!" Right, Da Da the Swedish kike lover, you bring me the straight tip, bung it to me.'

Dahlerus has described this encounter with Hitler as meeting a phantom from a story book. When he had told the Führer of the hard resolve not to countenance his aims, which had been formed by His Majesty's Government, and the probable consequences of any further aggressive action which the Führer might be contemplating,

Mr Dahlerus seems to have sparked off a fair old show of frantic auto-puppetry by Alf.

Erratically flinging his now bloated kisser back and then forward almost to the carpet, again and again and again, milling his arms in chopping great rings, heavily stamping his feet over and over and over, the Führer now began to bark in the voice that had captivated millions: 'U-boats! I shall build U-boats! Shall build U-boats! Build U-boats! U-boats! U-boats! U-boats! U-boats! I shall build U-boats!' There then followed a few phrases which Mr Dahlerus found that he couldn't follow at all but which, I fancy, went, 'It is my unshakeable intention to build a dog-track at Linz.'

Da Da looked at Fat Hermann, Hermann was just watching, nor did he wobble a chin.

Mr D has recalled that Hitler next asked him why England had perpetually failed to make an agreement with him. After Mr D had diffidently suggested that perhaps it might be that they did not hold complete confidence in either him or his party, Alf had stuck his livid face into Mr D's and shrieked, while at the same time banging his own left tit with his fist, 'Numbskulls! Have I ever told a lie in my life? Aeroplanes! I shall build aeroplanes! Shall build aeroplanes, build aeroplanes, aeroplanes! Aeroplanes! Aeroplanes! Aeroplanes! I shall build aeroplanes and I shall annihilate my enemies!'

IT WAS the middle of the May of 1940 when I joined my sister, mother and father in Hunsbeck, and the days were getting longer. Barrage balloons floated over the sandbagged streets. Over the tin hats and the gas masks, floated the big balloons. Over the soldiers, sailors, airmen. Over children, over parents, over sons and daughters, over dogs, cats, horses, air-raid wardens, firemen, clothing coupons, ration books, stirrup-pumps, friends, barbed wire and strangers, over all humankind in England floated those preposterous balloons.

As rats nests go, 15 Peartree Lane, Hunsbeck, hadn't been all that rough. Nothing could have been done about its size, the dirtiness of the little spot had been soon scrubbed away. An ingenious ramshackle arrangement had given us access to the back of our back-to-back, while at its front Mummy had made a hilarious machine for cooking, washing and supplying hot water by uniting the forces of cold water tap and sink, fire and oven, gas cooker and a glorious, five-gallon tea urn. A couple of armchairs, a sofa, a table, pretty lamps and a filled bookcase had given us a canteen, library and bathing hut. Going to the loo had been a bore. One had either to scuttle through the coal cellar for privacy at the back or share the one on the outside of the front with two other families. The nature of the errand had often been the decider. There had been a bedroom for my mother and father, a smaller one for my sister and, half-way up the stairs, a dainty little number for me. All in all, I have since seen, been and lived in far worse. Never, though, have I seen so many little houses piled in rows together, or anything so black filthy from industrial waste and soot. All the men, women and children of Hunsbeck had had to fight to be clean.

Our short street had abutted onto a wasteland of demolished houses at whose end ran a railway line which had also served as northernmost boundary to the district. A few doors to our right stood a permanently locked and shuttered small warehouse, fenced with iron-spiked tall slats of timber. Opposite, and a bit further on, was a pub which stood in a street of shops. There lived a former policeman, an acquaintance of my father. Behind the warehouse lived a ganger, a building-site foreman, a friendly Irishman, an honorary kinsman, call him Podge. To our left, one could either left, right, left again and right it to a main road and tram-stop, or carry straight on into a quaint, three-sided quadrangle where the local bookie had lived and functioned.

Our immediate neighbour had been the valorous Mr Spunk, body bent as a paperclip, two surgical-booted feet, his head thrust forward to about four feet from the ground, walking with a moving rocking motion, he had held his own as an unskilled labourer at an engine factory. Mr Spunk's house had been kept in gleaming nick by Rita, his quiet, shy and tidy wife who had always worn a ribbon round her short straight hair. They both cherished Ernest, a boy of my age, their straight-limbed son.

Close neighbours too had been the dwarf Harold, his older, taller, much thinner, toothless brother Raymond, both about thirty, both unskilled labourers, and the daddy, Old Tom, a retired unskilled labourer. Old Tom's wife, the boys' mother, had popped her clogs, died, some fifteen years earlier. Across the cobbles had lived a short, bald barrel of a man called Sammy, with legs bowed as a doughnut and a vast wife. They were childless, as was their immediate neighbour, Young Tom, a widower who had been poison-gassed in the First World War. A tall, white-haired, haggard man, Young Tom, whose frightening cough had hacked through the nights. He, too, had been an unskilled labourer.

None of these persons or places had been much remarked by me during my first short stay in Hunsbeck. What little I remember of that time includes my daddy's absences, my mother's determination to make things work, my room, my ship safely in it, and, disturbingly, a printed notice telling that Hitler would bomb and gas us without sending warning and we should therefore always carry our gas masks. Mine had become a sinister thing to me and I loathed it. 'The best time to attack is after the victory,' the Führer had said. By early 1940, mechanised, armoured and wheeled, his blitzkrieg had been staggering a continent.

Bloody man, Hitler. There had been real alarm among grown-ups in that May of 1940 and us children had sensed this; wrongs were going to be done for right reasons and you could smell it. At once, confusion and exhilaration.

Into all this popped Daddy.

Mystified by my mother's weeping, delighted to see the old bugger, we had shortly been wheeled out through Yorkshire's green lanes and dales of gilded broadacres up to the wilder fells and moors

of the North and into a small hotel in a village there; call it
Starsbottom. My memories of Starsbottom had deepened and
become defined by about my age of ten and have been often
refreshed there. One time, at Starsbottom, the sun had burned
down brightly for weeks. Dee, Wilf and I had been affeared of
dehydration and so had sipped quite a lot of electric soup. Evening
had come and hard pissing rain with it. Out of the cold wet sudden
night strode an upright, tall, tough old sheep farmer. From his
streaming, tanned and chopped sweet kisser a flat, bass hammer
of a voice had said, 'The fucking weather's turned honest.'

At Starsbottom my old daddy had laid new news on Constance
Jane. He'd spotted the half chance, do you see, dummied outside,
and then gone through the gap, leaving the opposition footing it
in the alternative direction. He had the ball at his feet, sweetheart,
was going to kick for touch and it was a hundred to plenty against
the draw.

War had meant that the British Government needed skilled
workers; Daddy was one such, rusty, woefully, but nothing that
a tune on the T-square and a bang with his hammer wouldn't fix.
Telling no one, he had applied for, and eventually been given, a
job as war-time Bodger to the Royal Navy. Working during the
weekdays in a restricted naval establishment at an inland town
on a river; pounding bits of ships into proportionate slabs, which
were then floated down the river, out into the open sea, scooped
up and assembled elsewhere. That had banjaxed everybody, family
and all, no one had known where the old bugger had been going
to or coming from. More, this work would mean modest but
steady trickles of wages, surely they would help to keep the SS
O'Toole afloat.

Mummy had been flabbergasted and enchanted to learn that
her husband was a craftsman. Patricia had gurgled, while I had
been rosily chuffed that my daddy would soon be punching his
weight in the war effort against Hitler.

A few days only we had shared that time at Starsbottom, days

45

when we had walked and splashed and climbed and romped and eaten and drunk and talked and scolded and squabbled and hushed and wept and chuckled as we had always done and would always do for all our lives, I, my sister and our mother and father.

There had been talk of German war planes, of bombs and of evacuation. France was falling, Czechoslovakia, Poland, Norway, Denmark, Belgium and Holland were gone, the British Expeditionary Force was on the run to the Channel ports and Dunkirk was approaching. The fear of massive German bombardment by armadas of enemy aircraft had been as real to some in England as the terror was to become in the appalling months that followed hard upon, when the great ranks of German war planes spilled their screaming bombs on our towns and cities, maiming and mutilating their populations.

Evacuation? That was all right by me, larky even, new parts in which to loiter, spreading sweetness and light. Later, an official fuss had been made, because one had left one's former district. Enter, into yet another building stuffed with those made pompously insufferable by office, Constance J. Scots wha hae wi Wallace bled and who cut like a knife when appropriately whetted.

While Connie was carving common sense, with its astonishingly pretty features, into the thick skull of some wretched Jack or Jill in office, Daddy and I had studied the posters stuck up there. Some concerned themselves with warning how careless talk could cost lives: one showed a cartoon drawing of Hitler hiding under a bus seat, earwigging the conversation going on above him. It made me smile. Daddy found one that made him pipe with laughter: Hitler lying full length on a railway-carriage luggage rack, earwigging. Were you ever in a first-class railway carriage filled with travelling, gambling men? The green baize table is easily provided: two small suitcases standing, a larger one laid flat, a towel placed over, and you're elected. The luggage rack is usually worth a peep. It is a point of protocol among the skint that, whatever the caste to which your bought ticket gives you entry, one should certainly travel first

class because one is an under-funded first-class person. At times
the approach of vigilant ticket collectors may prompt nimble
subterfuge among the racked-up bags, hats, coats and bookies'
brollies. If spotted, well, wait till the ship, card, coin, dog, horse,
bat comes in, you'll be boiling whiskey in the engine. One time you
might have found me, having a snooze, chugging contentedly from
Ponty to Donny. Years later, when I was a bell-bottomed sailor,
it was soon pointed out to me by hairy members from the crews
of the Royal Navy's smally boats, that when travelling inland for
hours and hours on a chuff-chuff, lying down is to be preferred to
either sitting or standing; therefore sling your hammock high up in
swaying corridors and spaces, or failing which, paste yourself flat
along the luggage rack.

Mummy had prevailed. One further visit had to be made: to
meet a bride of Christ and a nervous little plump lady, barely
taller than me, owlishly spectacled, who had seemed quite alarmed
when the two of us talked privately. It had been fixed. I would be
evacuated to a rural area in the Midlands. My billet would be
with a Mr and Mrs Terence Steeple. Their home was in George
Eliot and The Green Man Robin country. Mr Steeple was a miller
and Mrs Steeple a teacher of elocution and the pianoforte. Off to
the races.

MILLING WITH uniformed men and women, strewn with kitbags,
luggage, sleeping figures, freight and mailbags, the railway station
had chugged, whistled and steamed up hot on the day when I set
out for Lossborough.

The bony nun and the nervous little sausage of a lady had been
glimpsed all right but nothing much more of that day has stayed in
my mind. No leavetaking, no fear, no sadness. Solitariness, though,
alone or among others, sitting on a train, my name written on
a cardboard label stuck to my lapel with a safety-pin, one of

hundreds of thousands of children being sent out of the range of Hitler's bombers to a foster home somewhere deep in the English countryside.

After we had arrived at a dinky rural station, the nun and the sausage began bothering me about my bags, bossily telling me that I had brought more than had been advised. Now, I had with me only one suitcase, a holdall, my haversack and the bloody gas mask, so I could not understand their fuss, found it unreasonable, and so had sat on my few possessions, ripped out the hideous gas mask, stuck it on me and let yodel a few verses of 'She'll Be Coming Round The Mountain'. This had not gone down too well with either sausage or sister; had indeed, prompted tuts and shushes from them. I would not be shushed nor tutted; I would thus protect my jammies and my ship, my comics and my books, my green windjammer and my pistol.

Why, what would Merlin have done? Would he not have swirled his great cloak about him, have grown hugely, terrifyingly tall, have stood on a cliff-top, and would not then the sun have gone in? Away, you desperate women, I will sit on my belongings and sing through my gas mask. 'Yi yi yippee yippee yi.'

It had been while we were so occupied that the miller and his wife the elocutionist arrived to receive their charge. Unpeeled from my gas mask I sat before them. The miller, with grunts and bluff assurances, ushered away Sister Pilar Dolores and Mrs Sausage, while the elocutionist and piano teacher, a tall, darkly dressed, fair-haired woman wearing on her slim, hooky, mild features a pair of transparent pink-rimmed spectacles, bent down to me, bade me welcome and offered to help me carry my threatened effects.

Mr and Mrs Steeple, with me and my kit, had then walked out of the station and into the waiting bread van. Petrol had, of course, been strictly rationed but for those who delivered us each day our daily bread there had been an ample dispensation. With Mr Steeple at the wheel, Mrs Steeple and I sharing a front seat, I inhaling scents of warm, crisp, crusted loaves, Mrs Steeple gently chirruping of this and t'other, we set out through summery fields, over a hooped bridge spanning a broad, swift-running river and had eventually arrived at my foster home.

A neat-enough house in a trim village street. At its back stood a big wooden rain barrel which had immediately provided harbour for my ship and from where we looked out over a broad, long playing-field; cricket in its season, football in its. Idyllic it should have been but there had been snags. When the war began, Ralph, Mr and Mrs Steeple's only son, had volunteered for the army and had been killed in a freak accident. He had been sitting on the floor of a travelling army lorry, the lorry had bumped into a metal post, a tin hat had become dislodged, fallen heavily, its sharp brim had stabbed into the nape of Ralph's neck, had broken it and Ralph had died instantly. A photograph of their son, wearing spectacles remarkably like his mother's, had rested on the chimney-piece of the parlour and music room.

'Every Good Boy Deserves Fish,' intoned Mrs Steeple on the days when I had sat thumping away at the piano in that room. To this day, given a week or so for study and polishing, I could rest my music up on a piano and tinkle you off a 'Twinkle Twinkle Little Star' or a bar or two from one Brahms lullaby.

Indeed, one fine night, years later, delinquent and irresponsible, aflame with scrumpy, a venerable headmaster and I had broken into a venerable abbey, perched my music on the stand of the venerable organ, pulled out all the stops and, to my accompaniment, we had sung 'Twinkle Twinkle Little Star' in full voice and vibrato, giving, at three in the morning, a taste of our talent to a venerable English county.

The following afternoon the headmaster and I were in his garden practising fly-fishing with hookless rods and lines when the local police sergeant had shown up bearing news of last night's profane incident at the abbey. He had told the headmaster it was believed that a methylated spirits drinker and snowdropper, who had been sighted recently in the area, was responsible for this outrage. Snowdropping is the business of some poor sods who, often from laundry drying on a clothes line, pinch items of ladies' underwear, take them away and sniff them. Skid-row gutter-boozing being one thing, going to bed with a good pair of knickers being another, the two activities combined is a singularly unappetising body.

After the sergeant left, perhaps in pursuit of this perverse, sodden, organ-playing vandal, my friend the headmaster had wondered aloud to me, 'And to think, Peter, that it is not him,' then wristily flicking his rod, had added, 'Actus non facit reum, nisi mens sit rea,' which, he was good enough to explain to me, is Latin for, 'The act is not criminal unless the mind is criminal.'

———

DEAD RALPH'S room had been given to me. It was no mausoleum, there were no racks of deadman's clothes, no neat rows of shoes, no opened book but, still and all, what with poor Mrs Steeple going on quite a wistful bit about her dead son and Mr Steeple's respectful, stern silences during these unhappy flutings, Ralph had been beginning to fill up my skin. It is much plainer to me now than it could have been to the not quite eight year old me that I had been those days at Lossborough. The miller Mr Steeple and the piano teacher and elocutionist, Mrs Steeple, his wife, had been two peaceful civilians whom the war had made know loss and tragedy but who had added their small number to the many millions of generous, brave civilians who, more or less afflicted as Mr and Mrs Steeple, yet still had given refuge to strangers escaping from horror. This, in spite of the abominations committed daily by many other millions, here in slaughterous Europe between 1939 and 1945.

Attendance at the village school, too, had had its moments. The war had closed most schools in England, their younger members of staff in one way or another having joined in the prosecution of the war, those schools that remained open had been staffed by older teachers. The village school at Lossborough had, alas, remained open.

Mrs Steeple and I had entered through the scuffles and bustle of a classroom of schoolboys. My name had been elocuted to Mrs Blower, the only teacher of the only class in the only school at Lossborough, and appropriate introductions had been made to my schoolfellows, none of whom I remember. My remembrance of that first day at Lossborough village school is of Mrs Blower only. Mrs Blower: ruddy, pretty, fiercely spectacled, round and bumpy, dressed severely, her face fringed with dark grey hair, who had stared at me that day as if I had just stepped in off a passing moon.

On another day it had seemed right for me to offer to Mrs Blower for her consideration the plain fact that my being Catholic meant not only that I adhered to the One True Faith but also that in the true version of the Lord's Prayer the words differed from those uttered here at Lossborough. We had no 'For thine is the kingdom the power and the glory, for ever and ever' pumping on after 'deliver us from evil'; we simply honked 'Amen' and made an end. Which was what in future I proposed to do, in dread of sinning against the Holy Ghost, the presumption or despair prompted by quoting the alien, Lossborough version. More: they did not sing at Lossborough the Truetodeedle Song:

> 'Faith of our Fathers, Holy Faith,
> We shall be true to thee till death'.

A school which did not sing the Truetodeedle Song wanted the stirring faithful howl of being 'True to thee till death', was hardly worth turning up to, and so would Mrs Blower please have the goodness to point me in the direction of the nearest Catholic Church and away from all this fucking heathenry?

They had had no such sanctuary.

On yet another occasion it had been announced by Mrs Blower

that the morning would bring a day of celebration, when some false god or other would be praised, and that as it had been proposed to dish up a frightful, milky old jelly called junket to the school at an outing to be held in the fields down by the river, it would be meet that we should all pray to God to grant us fair weather tomorrow.

They had prayed to their God and I had prayed to mine.

Came the day of the race and it had solidly pissed down with rain all morning and well into the afternoon. Mrs Blower had called for silence and had said to us children that she was afraid that God had not answered our prayers. This had seemed to me at once daft, a misapprehension of the ways in which God moved, steaming mortal sin, and a matter which had needed an immediate rub down with *Sporting Life*.

God had answered our prayers, I had informed Mrs Blower: He had said no.

There had been a fuss. Disabused of her folly, Mrs Blower had expressed the firm view that she and her school could be of no further benefit to me. That's what it had boiled down to but what would Merlin have done? Would he not have turned into a great shaking oak tree, chuckling and pelting us with hard green acorns, then have changed us all into cats, before walking in human form to a cliff-top, and wouldn't the sun have then gone in?

SITTING WITH my back against the rain barrel, stroking my purring black cat. Inside the house a girl is under the tuning fork, giving us on the piano a touch of the Post Horn Gallop. The girl is not pleased. To play this piece properly one has to rap down briskly three precise series of tiddy-tums. One then firmly plonks in the crescendo, following this with a further row of tiddy-tums. Not this girl. The first hard sprinklings of tiddy-tums are being pressed in right enough but in place of the high tiddy-tum the girl is substituting a wonderfully loud displeased shriek.

What is that to Harry Beeste and me? Not a lot. We've heard it and its like before.

H. Beeste is a forbidden cat, one that is not welcome here. Whose cat he is, if anyone's, we do not know. He is a tomcat with no collar. Mrs Steeple says he stinks and Mr that he's filthy. So, too, would they stink and be filthy had they spent hard wet nights prowling through dustbins, torn at fish-heads, lost ears and nostrils fighting ferociously and fallen in love on the roof.

Four to a cow is a lot. One boy can usually sit on her for a while but when seating two the boy in front should tightly grab her horns. She will usually get quite frisky then and the difficulty of staying on her is multiplied by the difficulty of mounting up the other two. It's been done, of course, but only for a few seconds. Four is a lot to a cow.

Nor is flailing at the wasps' nest with your green windjammer to be too highly recommended. We were seriously slowed down when scrumping, thieving apples, by a boy who had been game but sluggish. When scrumping it is important to have some knowledge of the proposed booty. To know the rosy and the green when ripened, to pluck your swelling Cox's Orange Grandma not your stiff unready Grandad's Cock Cooking number, which can cost your tummy dear for days. This knowledge lends swiftness when plucking or picking; the hazardous stage of the operation.

Pockets, windjammer and gob stuffed with their choicest, the ascent back over the wall had been a breeze. Just a heave and a scrabble and a haul. True, Terence de Burgh had split the arse of his good trousers and I had copped yet another wound on the battlefield of a young boy's knee, but Eugene and Terence, the de Burgh brothers, and I were safely over. Mission nearly accomplished, a trot down the path, hop into the woods and, full of stolen apples, with gut ache and castor oil the prospect, we would be home and dried.

Richard had been nabbed. Sluggish in his ascent of the stone wall, the man from whose orchard we had been liberating apples had got him bang to rights.

Happily for Richard the man had had no dog.

Eugene had made a back for Terence, Terence had shimmied up on top of the wall. From there he had called to us that the man had got Richard in a half-nelson, his arms hooped around Richard's head, pressing him down. Eugene had said for me to make a back which I had staggeringly done. There had been one surprisingly heavy press from the sole of Eugene's boot, I had lurched and busted the other knee, but Gene was up. The pair of them had then had a cool conference about tactics, their strategy being clear: somehow to persuade Richard's captor to release him. Then they had both dropped back into the orchard.

Crouched under the wall, dispossessing myself of fruit, listening to their racket; their anger and their banter and their dangerous laughter, the threats, the thuds, whimpers, yells and the feet running hard.

Here's a perplexity, now; here's a bafflement, here is fear. To skedaddle sharpish through the trees and away? To quiver whimpering where I crouch? To leap up the wall, grab the top with my hands, arms and elbows, scramble sideways with my feet and then somehow heave myself up in the way that the big boys do? What to do? Terry and Gene have gone back for Richard; I huddle here and quake; there is quite nothing left of my knees now. Ordinarily the state of my wounded knees is a tickle point of vanity with me, holding, as I do, the view that the damage done to his knees by a boy is usually quite honourably copped, may be worn with open dignity, much as one might wear a medal, and is not to be considered just showing off. Not this lot. They are wholly crocked, these knees. They are all blood and shite and indentations; they are guilty, fearful and wobbling things; battered knockers that scarce hold me up as at last I rise and stand, wondering what shall I do. Shouldn't I be with Gene and Terry fighting for their own and sluggish Richard's lives? Technically, yes; but even if I could get to them I greatly don't want to; and it's not the bloodying of noses that's deterring me, it's the dread of being caught. Scoot down the lane and the straight way through the leaves to be rid of myself? Charming thought but not acceptable: it would be yellow. Quiver on here doing nothing at all save dread all possibilities, deeply concerned that, should this bungled heist yet have mercy in it, the gruesome state my knees are in will call for hard questions?

Sir Yvain is in the Land of Gore petting his toothless old lion; the orchards of Lossborough may be blue with plodding constabulary; and I'm on the verge of throwing a wobbler during the de Burgh and Company apple caper.

There is a barking sound of tough and sturdy boys. Down my path from a side turning, going like a Derby winner, Richard the Slug comes hurtling ahead of the cantering, chuckling de Burgh brothers. They glance behind to see who dares follow them, but no one does. They boot me on in front of them as though I were a ball and we put quick distance between ourselves and the angry applejack.

It's the shape and size of a rugby ball but whitish grey of colour and stuck under the lid of a mechanised well dug just before the soccer pitch beyond the churchyard. What can it be? Now, because I was barely eight, the de Burghs ten and eleven and Richard almost twelve, my chief value to the outfit was that of utility member, handy for a mounting block or a ball retriever or a goalpost even. Thus I was elected investigator of large egg-shaped objects unexpectedly sticking out of wells.

Richard's advice to kick it was paid no heed; it might be an unexploded bomb or an aerial torpedo, you never knew; or a meteorite. Hot it was and we had run far, nor was my fright completely gone. The man had not been struck hard, nor bruised to death with fusillades of bright apples, but, frightened just by the menace of Terence and Eugene, he had let Richard go.

Now I'm flushed, sweating and thirsty and there is this ovoid to consider. Round my waist, tied by its arms, the green windjammer droops. Round the well the black and yellow of a wasp angrily grinds through the air. As much to protect myself from stings as to flog at the mysterious object, my windjammer was untied, and then gingerly the flickings began. One of my casts was heavily accurate and the big egg tilted. Encouraged by it not exploding, my pin point targetry and instructions from the elders of my firm, I gave it another swipe of the corduroy jacket. Amazed and horrified I goggled as from the body of the egg tumbled scores of wasps crawling, scrambling, flying furiously to teem in a raging dark flock which suddenly flung itself at my eyes.

It is said that Duffy was the fastest man ever over a hundred yards. Duffy had been a great champion of the professional Powderhall sprints in the early nineteenth century. His exact times are not known but the Powderhall was a handicap event. The handicappers set the mean time for the distance at ten seconds. The prized 'even time': ten yards every second. Slower runners had a mark up the stretch from the start, running less than a hundred yards, the faster runners had a mark behind the start, running more than a hundred yards. My old Pop had been given five yards' start as his mark when he ran in the event, but the long ago Duffy's mark was eleven yards behind the start. That's one hundred and eleven yards. 'Off Duffy's mark', a phrase still used by The Fancy suggesting someone who is severely handicapped. To catch, pass and win from an even timer he would have had to clock over the hundred eight point nine seconds. Which the position of his mark suggests that he did. That's travelling.

A new mark would have been needed for Duffy had he been able to catch me on the day that I had been elevated to the post of explorer and disturber of a nest of wasps.

A Powderhall and more away, the rest of the team had eventually trotted up to where I lay puffed and giddy with relief. Seconds before I had believed I would be stabbed to death with stings from dozens of black and yellow brutes, that there were wasps

Constance Jane Eliot Ferguson (Mrs. P. O'Toole)
Yorkshire, England, 1939.

clambering through my ears to dart around inside my face, but now they were not, nor had I been stung, the wasps all were gone.

So, too, was my green windjammer with the gold-plated zip fastener.

Often, sitting with my back to the rain barrel, I had fancied myself when wearing it to be Sir Ivaine, son of Queen Morgan Le Fay, nephew of King Arthur, my own hero and favourite knight of the Round Table.

The green and golden windjammer now lay dropped and lost at the Well of the Wasps, my fellow Knights of the Scrump Perilous lay reluctant for a return sally, Sir Yvain was not available, so I had to shuffle alone back to Sting City and try to scoop up the wretched article.

Twenty or so yards from the well and the scene there was horrible. The jacket was on the ground below the nest but the place was alive with very cross wasps indeed, bitter about the buffets given to their home and well-being and keen to find sweet, bad boys to sting.

Terry and Gene had arrived at my side and may have seen my distress at this predicament. Gene had pulled his shirt into a hood over his head, had held it there with one hand, had walked stooping back to the well, had been stung on his arms, legs and stomach, had picked up my windjammer, had moved rapidly with it from the well, flung it victoriously at my feet and shouted, 'Tooley, you're a dozy pillock. Next time don't drop it.' He then fetched me a surprising box on the left ear which had fair made it chime.

Gingerly sidefooting my jacket along, fearful lest wasps lurked in it, I had watched Gene and Terry bowling away, cursing warmly, brightly prattling, their arms around each other, and had heard them laugh their odd, easy laughter.

———————

FOUR YEARS later, and the war still bloodily rolling on, chance found Terence, Eugene and me attending the same school. I was present when an enraged and formidable teacher had said of the brothers that they would either build an empire or be hanged.

Castle Catholics from Leinster, the family de Burgh had moved to England in 1937. Brainy, stormy and likeable, father had signed up for war work when the balloon went up in 1939. Very like father indeed, his sons, they had eventually been evacuated to Lossborough where they had spread an impudent, cheerful havoc whose splinters I had touched. Dark complexions, dark curly hair, wide, bright black eyes; big, bustling, stocky boys in short trousers, open-necked shirts, usually with fags in their gobs, and always with their socks around their boots. After our unexpected reunion at school in 1944, our families remained in occasional touch for a number of years. My last recollection of being with them is when I was sixteen or so. Terence has spent most of his adult life in prisons of all sorts; Gene was hanged in an African prison in the middle fifties: he had taken a pair of workroom shears to a warder he didn't much fancy and had snipped him to death. As Jack Jack said to me that night when we had chuntered together late and deeply in the Dales, 'Gene. Topped. It would be nice to think that he'd kicked the hangman in the balls, but one doubts it.'

'PUT THE cloths and clothes in the clothes basket and close the clothes basket.' Try that till you're sick of the sound and saying of it and make articulate, splashless distinctions between the Z, T, Th and S sounds, while at the same time keeping your teeth together, tapping lightly with the tip of your tongue against both the soft and hard palates and your upper clenched gnashers. You will presently get a hint of what being a pupil of Mrs Steeple had been like. 'Two ghosts sat on posts drinking toasts to their hosts.'

As these events are being shuffled around in my mind, pictures of Mr Steeple clearly present themselves. A large, bulky, taciturn man who seldom spoke; indeed, nothing that he had said remains with me. Sometimes we passed each other in the street, at times I would see him sitting silently in his chair, other times he would be leaning on the fence looking over the playing field, his back to the house, a hand supporting his chin, just gazing, saying nothing. Perhaps my being there had irked him, perhaps he had been musing quietly of his dead son, perhaps it had been merely his habitual manner, but he stays with me; a lumbering, dour and melancholy man.

Rare enough to recall had been his smiles.

The river at Lossborough is tidal and presents in its season a natural phenomenon: a swelling wave running rapidly past the banks, under the bridges, around the bends and all along the length of the broad, deep river.

Mr Steeple and I had motored out in the bread van to a rocky vantage point, overarched with trees, where we would get a close sight of this splendid event. A hump the width of the river had appeared a distance away, rolled tumbling towards us, spraying and churning had passed us, and had then gone bowing away to arc around a farther bend. Lovely. I had looked up at Mr Steeple, Mr Steeple had stood there gazing at where the wave had gone, gently nodding his head, and with a crusty smile on his sad old face.

At meals Mrs Steeple had introduced me to a custom which had baffled me. A small portion of each course, be it starters, main or pudding, had had to be left on our plates for 'Mr Manners'. Why Mr Manners, or anyone else, should find being left a forkful or so of cold Brussels sprout to be both proper and polite flummoxed me then as much as it would do now. Nevertheless, it had been the daily ritual to leave genteel lumps of our war-rationed grub sitting on the crockery, an offering to good Mr Manners.

One day, perhaps a day on which I was replete with still obtainable, wholly scrumptious Liquorice Allsorts, Dandelion and Burdock and the endlessly chewable Treacle Toffee, we sat down at table where, after they had said their grace and I had said mine, Mrs Steeple piped out the forthcoming menu, say, mulligatawny soup, braised tongue and cabbage, followed by figs and custard. Nothing there had much struck my fancy nor had seemed to me to be a patch on Peardrops, Coconut Mushrooms or Penny Dabs and so I had suggested to Mrs Steeple that rather than leave Mr Manners only fragments of our fare we should give him in advance the entire issue, parsnips and all. Clucking darkly, I fancy, of how this Baal of mealtime etiquette could not be so crudely propitiated, Mrs Steeple had fluttered into the kitchen. Snuffling grunts of a queer sort were being made by Mr Steeple and so I had looked at him expecting a censorious glower. No: his eyes closed, shoulders slightly shaking, chin on chest, he had been enjoying a modest squirt of mirth. Bearing the tureen, Mrs Steeple had re-entered the room. Mr S had coughed, opened his eyes, clutched his spoon and, before doing measured justice to his broth, had given me a look of what I believe to have been quiet, conspiratorial fun.

———————

OBADIAH WAS his name, the village idiot, his face would have suited well as the features of a goblin drawn by Dadd the painter and patricide. An old, young, withered boy, for ever isolated in his world, under a cloth cap and a roomy overcoat in those hot summer days, his hands continually describing, moulding, framing the argument that his mind could not utter through his open, mute mouth. My first sight of him had been at a village cricket match. Ignored by the few spectators there, he had been wandering round the boundary, pausing now and then to play a batsman's stroke, to make an umpire's signal, to turn a bowler's arm, to take a fielder's catch.

Rumour had spoken of him living in a dog kennel behind a builder's yard over the bridge but I had found nothing to be doggy or dirty about him and it became our habit, Obadiah's and mine, to meet by the hedge surrounding the rectory and to walk a short while along a path which led to a turning where I would peel off to go in for my tea and Obadiah would stroll on conducting his ceaseless and silent conversations. Each time that we met Obadiah would greet me by turning his arms in front of him, making two large circles which I knew to mean 'hello', and when we parted he would stretch his arms straight ahead and then twice wave them up and down, which I knew meant 'goodbye'. During the course of our short rambles I would chatter of this and that, Obadiah would listen, at times wrinkling his brows, at times mouthing unspoken words, at all times orchestrating appropriate gestures.

One evening I had spotted Obadiah being led into a nearby pub by a group of heartily bucolic, loud young men, some of whom had been in uniform. After supper, feeling strangely uneasy, I had nipped over the fence, circled round the field, and had popped out near to where the pub stood. Songs and shouts and bellows of laughter were coming from the pub. Through a clear slice of a frosted-glass side window I could see into the bar. Around the dartboard a circle of men was grouped, in the centre stood Obadiah wearing cap and overcoat, a pint of beer in one hand, in the other hand a dart.

A red-faced fat man hoisted up the hand in which Obadiah held the pot of beer and then holding him by the back of the neck, slowly the fat man thrust Obadiah's face into the froth. Obadiah gulped, spluttered, grimaced, beer slopped down his face, overcoat and onto the floor. Again and again his face was thrust into the pot, more and more was Obadiah gulping, grimacing, spluttering, more and more beer was slopping down as loud cheers and yells of boozy encouragement were being offered by his hosts.

Obadiah stands holding the empty pint pot by its handle as though it were a suitcase and aiming his dart at the board. The group scatters away from the line of fire, some under tables, some ducking behind stools, all whooping with glee. Slowly and elaborately Obadiah winds his arm several times in the approved aiming and throwing position, stands quite still, his dart poised before his eyes, and then swiftly walks up to the dartboard deliberately to prod his dart right into the red bullseye in its centre.

How long my stay had been when peering through that pub window I don't know. Long enough to have heard the jeers of dismay after Obadiah's triumphant marksmanship. Long enough to have heard the singing of 'We're Going To Hang Out The Washing On The Siegfried Line' as Obadiah had been pushed around the pub, one man to another, punctuating the words. Enough time to have seen Obadiah's cap snatched off, to have noticed his well-combed hair with a centre parting, to have watched him hopelessly trying to grab at his cap as it was being skimmed around and up and down and across the room. Long enough, at last, to have seen the revellers tire of their baiting and, bored with him, to have given Obadiah the bum's rush through the door, out into the lane, throwing his cap after him.

He was sitting on the pavement when I approached him, his bottom on the kerb, his feet on the road, his cap back on his head, deep in lone communion, his hands and fingers shaping out his thoughts. 'Obadiah, it's me,' I said. He turned towards me, made his circles of greeting and then I looked into his face. His eyes were shining with a great happiness; his mouth spreading out softly into a deeply contented grin. 'Goodnight,' I had said. Obadiah had waved me his goodbyes.

———

> Cats on the rooftops, cats on the tiles,
> Cats with syphilis, cats with piles,
> Cats with their arseholes wreathed in smiles,
> As they revel in the joys of fornication.

HARRY BEESTE'S nose was split something shocking, one ear was buckled, a hank of hair had been gouged out from the top of his tail and he was gloomy and generally ill-disposed towards the morning world. Nor would he suffer me to stroke him but he had roughly tongued down a few fingerfuls of condensed milk, had gobbled the chunk of cheese to which he had lately become accustomed and was now snoozing at my side as I sat at the rain barrel pondering the possible course of the river that I had seen yesterday.

There had been an excursion by coach for the families lodging evacuees and Mrs Steeple had taken me on the trip. Nothing of the journey had proved remarkable to me until the driver announced that we were passing a stream that ran into a river which flowed into Sherwood Forest. Immediately I wanted to leap from the vehicle, jump into the stream and paddle its length into the greenwood haunts of Robin, Scarlet, Little John, Mutch, Alan and Michael Tuck the friar. Dissuaded from this I had had to sit down on my seat and to settle for my waking dreams of bows and broadswords, daggers and quarterstaves, archery, fencing, combat, comradeship and troupes of outlawed men roaming through the trees.

Sitting now with Sir Harry, my friend the wounded night prowler, the notion came to me that the river was probably the one that famously streamed through Robin's secret winter cave. North of Sherwood, the cave is. At the bottom of a slope there is a rock covered all with creepers. You lightly press a point on the rock face and, as though on hinges, the boulder slowly spins round and you can enter into the cave. Light comes into the huge cave from cracks in the rock above, through it runs a clear, clean stream. A hundred and more outlaws can safely winter there and there is a labyrinth of small caves leading away from the main one which has many ledges and alcoves and cosy nooks. One cave is the armoury, there the swords are kept sharpened and polished, the arrows fitted with goose feathers and new steel tips and the bowstrings rubbed with tallow. Another is the hospital, clean soft beds are there, bandages and honey for to soothe the outlaws' wounds. Another is where the disguises are kept: horsehair wigs and beards; flock humps for hunchbacks; wooden legs, hooks for hands, and skirts and hoods for when the men dress up as women. There are places to bathe, places to sleep, a treasury, a kitchen, a banqueting hall and in one of the caves there is a chapel where Friar Tuck says Mass and bids Robin and his men remember another outlaw from long ago, who rode a donkey and was crowned with thorns, sweet, bold Jesus in Jerusalem.

'Peter,' a voice is calling deep into my reverie. 'Peter, son.'

It's my Daddy.

Daddy is standing there, wearing a large black hat, smiling and calling out my name. Daddy has come to take me away from here, to hold me and to hug me and to kiss me and to listen to me, to play with me, to pick me up and to whirl me round and to let me wear his fine, new, broad-brimmed, soft black hat.

No packing, no goodbyes, no farewells to Lossborough, nothing of my last few minutes there stays to murmur on in my memory.

We had motored off to Nottinghamshire, not, I fancy, as marauders for the Green Man to ambush the Sheriff there, but to have a day at the races. Whose car it had been, who had driven it, who had sat in the front, I don't know, but, fizzing with happiness, I had sat at the back tucked between Daddy and a newcomer to me, Jim the Waiter, a small, knotty, friendly man who had really seen and, better still, had actually fought German soldiers and who had survived and escaped from Dunkirk.

This had enthralled me for, yes, he had been dive-bombed by Stukas, of course he had pulled out the pins and hurled hand grenades, certainly he had crawled through the mud wearing camouflage and a tin hat, without doubt he had fixed a bayonet on his rifle, to be sure he had shot Nazis, seen the big tanks rolling, watched and heard the huge artillery guns booming out their shells, marched, saluted, countermarched and dived for cover, no, he had not been wounded, yes, he had friends who had been, yes, he had seen soldiers die, no, they had not surrendered, Dunkirk had been a tactical withdrawal.

When our car finally arrived at the track it had been translated into a heavily armoured vehicle and dozens of Nottinghamshire punters were lying dead or seriously wounded, machine-gunned down by me, the rear gunner, blown to bits by Jim with his mortar, or incinerated by my old Pop with his trusty flame thrower.

It was smashing to be back among the throng of gamesters, gee-gees, jockeys, bookies; the wide, white-railed dipping rails of the track, the gaudy brollies, chalkboards and beer tents, the raw hubbub of odds shouted, bets made, bets taken, whoops of winners, oaths of losers, hot tips, sure things, dead certs; all the calls and cries of racing men backing their fancies.

Pop not being up on the stool was a golden bonus; free to potter where we willed, with our new companion Jim the Waiter, we toured the bars and tents and stands, nodding here, chatting there, studying our cards, making our bets, urging on our choices.

An old china, china plate, mate, of my father's, a bookie whose pitch was far down the rails, away from the communal water tap and who we were visiting, couldn't successfully rub off his board the chalked-up odds from previous races: his sponge was dry, water wasn't handy and his mood was touchy. During the course of our perambulation I had with me a bottle of white lemonade from which I'd been having refreshing swigs and which I now offered up to my Daddy's friend as a possible solvent for his chalky difficulties. The lemonade had been taken, used and it had worked.

This had pleased me, but what had pleased me more was the bookie lifting me up, plonking me on his shoulders, holding me sitting up safely there, his big arm round my legs, and announcing to friends, customers and anyone listening that this young boy up here is Pat O'Toole's son, resourceful and generous as his father, a credit to the name and the game, destined, surely, to hold his own and more among the high-stepping horse fanciers who in time would tread The Turf.

For too long a time I had been regarded only as an invalid or an outsider, as reluctant lodger or infant heretic, and no Caesar returning to Rome for his triumph could have been tickled more pink than I had been that day when I was hoisted aloft to be praised for my timely ingenuity in offering up a few drops of pop to rub clean a bookie's chalkboard. Later, my disappointment that the ancient great range of Sherwood Forest no longer reached out to this Nottinghamshire racetrack, or, if it did, was represented now only by a dusty bush and a lamp-post, was being assuaged by a mug of tea and a thick slab of buttered bread spread dripping with strawberry jam. I was holding it to my mouth, gnawing contentedly at the deep lusciousness, when a wasp had flown purposefully, busily, swiftly in my direction. Whether or no the animal was an evacuee from a broken home at Lossborough, a stowaway perhaps, on my ship which had voyaged here safely in the boot of the car and who was now at liberty, I had no way of telling, but the beast had homed in directly on my jam butty, landed safely on my upper lip and had stung it.

THE KING is in the garden practising pistol shots, at Compiègne the Führer struts a jig. A banner of shadows hangs in swastikas over Europe, Tall Charles of France flies to England with the resistance flame and through the Arc de Triomphe the Huns on Horseback trot. Winston the Warrior of Marlborough's kin offers us nothing save blood, toil, tears and sweat but we shall meet the sword with sword and battle on alone. Hurricanes howl around the Fokkerwolves above our heads on Eagle's Day as Spitfires dogfight Messerschmitts and brave men meet their finest hour and die. The last race was run at Nottinghamshire, Daddy and

I set out for Hunsbeck, Merlin stood on the edge of a cliff, and the sun went in.

> And I say to you who have seen war like a wasp . . .
> Worse things shall be than have been.
> But they shall yet be better.

'I, Anna Csillag, with my six-foot-long Lorelei hair'.

THE SIREN who sang that song meant not to lure sailors onto her fatal rock but to persuade passersby to invest their pennies in a hair tonic. The words are from an advertisement floated by Frau Csillag of Vienna promoting what benefits would obtain from visiting her hair clinic, or, indeed, merely massaging into one's scalp at night a cupful or two of her matchlessly restorative snake oil. Sitting archly over the wording is a drawing of a Lorelei-like lady, maybe Frau Csillag herself, her two yards of tresses duly tumbling down. Throughout this century the clinic with this advertisement has adorned Vienna, it may do so still, who knows, but in 1911, when the lad was twenty-two, it had slapped itself bang into the eye and mind of Alf.

Astonished, outraged, delighted and thoughtfully had our Alf stared at, and then talk, talk, talked of, this poster with its brazenly improbable implications, expressing it to be the very stuff of propaganda. His dodgy mate at the time, Grudger Greiner, has said that Alf had gone on something alarming about propaganda. 'Propaganda! Propaganda! Propaganda!' he said over the chocolate cakes, cream cakes, tea and free newspapers in one of those dainty tearooms where young Hitler had spent most of his waking life, 'Propaganda is the fundamental essence of every religion, whether of heaven or hair tonic. You must keep it up until you build a faith

67

in which people no longer know what is imagination and what is reality.' Whatever he may have bent Greiner's ear with, or the ears of others, long cauliflowered by his musings in the Reading Room of the men's hostel where Adolf Hitler had chosen to lodge, he later made plain his views on the art of propaganda when he wrote *Mein Kampf*. It is the only chapter in that dirty great thick book that I have nearly read. That and a whiff of the Song of Syphilis, his own noisome threnody on the clap, found in the same volume. *Mein Kampf* would not be written for many years, not until after Hitler had been jailed as an armed insurrectionist and usurper of the lawful government of Bavaria.

At the age of twenty-two, Alf had lived four years in Vienna, and until recently had seldom needed to scrape a crust on which to live. He had taken ample care of that. Alf aged eighteen, Gustle, nineteen, both heavily provincial, had come down from Linz to the ferment of Vienna in its last years as capital city of the monarchy of Emperor Franz Josef, both to lead lives there as scholar Bohemians, with Alf as art student, Gustle as pianist and scholar of music.

Gustle had passed his entrance examination and taken up the work conscientiously, Alf had blown his; but he had been advised by a note from his examiners that, should he choose to pick up a few State Secondary Education Certificates attesting to advanced merit in academic disciplines other than drawing, at which he wasn't bad, then next year he might chance his arm at the Academy of Architecture.

Alf had been sorrowfully short of such fine documents. Had, in fact, had none. One knows the feeling. Cracks in an academic record cannot long be papered over with your RADA diploma and a certificate for swimming twenty-five yards. Alf, however, had cunningly mustered his resources and had fixed a nifty little swindle on the Linz Education Committee.

Because his cousin his mother had recently died, his father her uncle having predeceased his niece, Alf's mother, by four years, the fruit of their loins, Adolf Hitler, would be entitled to a substantial chunk of change from an orphan's pension if he was a genuine student of State Higher Education. Little Hitler had somehow weasel-wangled it. Alf had copped the pension and he was already drawing a steadily liquid financial inheritance from both his dead parents. Hitler had drawn enough to satisfy the needs and perhaps some of the wishes of a professional man of modest attainments, enough on which to keep a middle-class family going.

Gustle moved his piano into their shared digs beside the railway station which had seen their debouche from Linz and Alf indulged his notions of higher education. Excursions into Babylon were handy so Alf and Gustle sauntered out among the capes and canes of opera audiences, saw productions of Wagner's works performed over and over again, joined libraries, wondered at Viennese architecture, occasionally ate at restaurants, went to the cinema and, Alf in particular, found demi-paradise in cafés which were not dear, provided chocolate cakes, cream cakes, tea, free newspapers and had encouraged conversation.

When the nights drew in, Alf sketched, suggested improvements on public buildings at Linz, gabbled of writing a play, indeed, had gabbled out all his know-all gobshite to his sole friend and audience, Gustle, who, when let, would dutifully perform on the piano his novice's music practice. Fairly comfortable, musically and talkatively, they had thus shared a room by a railway station at Vienna.

WHEN WE arrived in London to commence our lives as scholar Bohemians, O'Liver and I had shared the bandstand at Green Park. Our treasury at that time, when we were both aged twenty, had held a couple of quid apiece and a crisp fiver that I had recently extorted from a loving relative. This we had happily blown on beer, pork pies, whiskey and good seats at *Guys and Dolls*.

69

'It's the only established, permanent floating crap game
in New Yor-or-or-ork.'

Glorious hymn to Runyon, it is. Harry the Horse, Nicely Nicely
Johnson, Bat, Adelaide, Nathan Detroit and all being played out
of their skins by that brilliant cast.

My heart had gone to Sam Levene as Nathan. My actor's
admiration for his playing remains an undimmed joy to me. Mr
Levene gave, uniquely, his form and pressure to the age and body
of Detroit's time, which would have pleased my lord Hamlet who
wisely instructs us actors to do just that, and moves me to consider
Sam Levene's playing of Nathan to be one of the great classical
performances of our time. Also, were ever adenoids so gainfully
employed as when Vivian Blaine so tunefully twanged them in
her lyrically comic 'Adelaide's Lament'? Was ever a threnody so
achingly well sung whose subject was a catarrhal upper respiratory
tract? Unlikely, I fancy. Who recalls the haunting mystery of a song
not included in the excellent film version of the play, which had
been sung to the Salgash lass by her Salgash dad?

Standing there gazing at me, full of the bloom of youth,
Standing there gazing at me, with a sheep's eye and a
    liquorice tooth.

After the curtain call, the cheers, applause and the encores, O'Liver
and I, softly howling to each other snippets of the words and
melodies from *Guys and Dolls* had swayed back to our residence
in the dim and leafy Green Park and had thought not of tomorrow,
our priority being getting through another night. We had sat on
our veranda, killed the half-bottle of whiskey and, contented, had
arranged ourselves for sleep.

O'Liver, the painter, two yards and more of long bones,
wild unweeded hair, peridot eyes, fluently combative speech and
whirling white long-fingered gestures, had the happy knack of
being able to topple on the spot where he had formerly stood

standing and pitch himself into untroubled sleep, no matter
what surface supported the snoring bundle of him. Not I. My
two years as salt-water sailor had taught me the art of kipping
anywhere, certainly, but also of kipping comfortably. Not for me
the ungiving, splintered wooden deck of an oompah bandstand.
Oh no. Canvas deckchairs for the comfort of their customers had
been marshalled by me into an erection which combined an artfully
arranged, yielding canvas and timber floor with a stout roof against
the uncertain elements. Surely much better than having a hipbone
ground to chalk by tiles, planks, stones and wet grass of the
bandstands, bus stations, ledges, benches, underneath the arches
and the green patches where the shelterless often doss.

Before crashing into coma, O'Liver had watched with amused
scorn my labours of construction, had seen me slither into my
bivouac, had heard me pronounce it good, had, I fancy, remarked
the night's stillness, heard the Fugue for Tinhorns singing in
his head, arranged his evening thoughts, chosen to dream on a
merrily seditious one and had prepared himself for to crumble into
unconsciousness.

Buy the bastard strong drink and even today O'Liver will tell
you that next on the programme he had heard a gurgled and
almighty roar from within my house of deckchairs, had seen an
explosion of timber and canvas with me levitating up from the pile
of it, beating myself brutally, hawking, heaving, snatching at my
flesh, retching, and, on landing, jumping up and down and rapidly
describing circles.

Snug enough had it been under there; serene and cosy,
comfortable and safe. However, without my knowledge, every
caterpillar and other herbivorous slitherer fat with the leaves,
grass and petals of Green Park, had chosen to spend the night
on a deckchair which had later become an indispensable section
of my roof. Unhappy, perhaps, at being so used, clinging on upside
down to my ceiling which had not given them the purchase needed
to snooze on, they had collectively decided to drop at once their

slimy bloated hairy bodies off my roof and flop themselves into the face and open mouth of the foreign body stretched out beneath them crooning 'Sue me, sue me, shoot bullets through me, I love you'. A mouthful of wriggling overfed caterpillars can stop one in mid vowel sound; a hairy little writher lodging on the windpipe can immediately start up the noise again with howling, spluttering variations.

O'Liver is one who when laughing does actually fall about and no brass instruments had been needed to liven up the midnight bandstand. Covered in caterpillars, uncorking myself of one, plucking out many from the hair, from the trunk through my opened shirt, grasping at the hairy bastards stamping around down my trousers, frantically I had had to strip and rid myself of the insufferable beasts, all to the accompaniment of O'Liver's hootings, clatterings about, sobs of laughter and repeated tossings of himself onto the dogshelf there, crudely raving, 'They bite! Caterpillars do bite! Throw him to the caterpillars!'

Morning came and after putting our last few bob on a wash and brush up at a railway station, with a cup of tea and a bun, we had sat in solemn deliberation and realised well that we would have to find work.

There is a time in the life of every bum when he will either stagnate where he lolls or rise and shine having mustered up a ring of bright shillings. The former condition cannot be postponed for long, the latter is often achieved by grabbing a handle of the implement and setting out to shovel all sorts of shit. Cement, snow, sand, green, picked peas, washing dead bodies, climbing steeples, demolishing *pissoirs*, all the fun of odd and heavy burdens lifted when young to subsidise one's scholarship and debauchery.

O'Liver had gone north, painted little but shovelled lots: green peas into sacks for their last journey before being put into a tin. He had scraped hard for his crust, had earned a pocketful of wages when, alas, sweating through the pea dust, a disagreement with a black colleague had led O'Liver to defend himself by arranging his shovel on the black man's head. An angry scene with the boss had followed and, even though his attacker had made a complete recovery, O'Liver had been dismissed from the pea-shovelling service. This, as you might imagine, had been no great hardship to him, and very shortly he had gone back to a life of daubing and lechery. I had gone muling with a pack of Paddies, humping sacks of cement into a concrete mixer, laying the foundations for an electrical power station. It had been lump work: paid for how much you do, you do a lot, the lorry picks you up under the clock at 7 a.m., nine hours later you finish if you wish or go on through the night if you are able; double headers, double bubble, thick wages and minimum regulations. A stake at my disposal to cushion the vital, uncertain months ahead of me had been important. Earlier that year had seen me take a short voyage on a one way liberty boat from the depot ship, call her the Montplonk, we did, of the submarine flotilla in which I had served for well over a year.

IT WAS not Royal Naval policy to take on board the compulsorily conscripted youths enjoined by law to do National Service; but they had made exceptions. Most of His Majesty's ships, from smally boats to battlewagons, had had to suffer one or two of these exceptions, and we special entry National Service seamen had moved diffidently at first among their crews of long-serving professional sailors, many of whom had fought in the sea battles of the war. Some of us had worn bell-bottoms, others square rig; some, better qualified, had bitten the bullet, become commissioned education officers, served three instead of the stipulated two years, taught hairy-arsed stokers long division and played rugby; others who had earnestly proved that they were seriously thinking of the Royal Navy as a profession had been heaved on board training ships, while yet others sailed as midshipmen and, being neither Pig nor Lower Deck, had been roundly abused by all sections

of the floating community. One small heap had worn badges
of crossed flags with the legend 'Coder E' above them; all the
wearers had been very clever indeed, but no one, certainly not
my friendly Coder E, had had the ghost of a notion of what their
duties precisely were. At times, my Coder E lay in his hammock,
the score of a Beethoven quartet in his hand, silently reading and
conducting its music; sometimes, when let, being cello and fiddle.
Passages from great *Lear* he had read to us, when the *Montplonk* hit
some choppy water and the weather had been brisk.

My friend Egg had sported a badge with an electrical spark on
it, signifying that he was a telegraphist, one who knew the Morse
code and how to receive and to transmit it. Doubtlessly he had been
so skilled but my chief recollection of him is his ability to sit down
when lightly scrubbing the deck. That and his excellent bullocking
about in the pack when ashore playing our plug-ugly rugby. The
crossed flags with no legend above on the badge that I had worn
meant that I was a signalman, one who knew the semaphore code
and how to receive and to transmit it. Certainly, this had been
one of my studies at the signal school which Egg and I had both
attended but fortunately not once during my time at sea had I ever
been asked to demonstrate this skill. Instead, I had blundered into
wanking a teleprinter, dashing around with messages and generally
making myself helpful to all while stationed at the signals office on
the bridge. On the left side of the office there had been a large
locker with a porthole; into this metal cupboard the volumes of
King's Regulations and Admiralty Instructions, I and the teleprinter had
been stowed. Under the books and the machine I had slid the camp
bed that was to be my berth for many months as the *Montplonk* rode
and bellied and heaved herself through the big old sea.

My sea had been black; black and grey with great lumps of
roaring white water crashing over our bows to rush swilling along
the lurching deck. Often I had stood, gloved hands gripping a rail
or a stanchion, just gazing, awed by this immense world of black
and brutal water. Northern waters had been our lot, and from the

74

Western Isles of Scotland we had sailed out through the Atlantic, the Irish Sea, the North Sea, the Pentland Firth, the Skagerrak, the Kattegat, the Baltic Sea and the Gulf of Bothnia. Nippy it had usually been, with rough weather the main feature, but there had been times of stillness, times of friendship, times of thoughtfulness, vigorous times, uncertain times, hilarious times and times of wonder and great beauty.

My days spent at shore establishments, though relieved by the occasional prank, had been often an irksome bother to me, but the days at sea and the nights and days when ashore in port, home or abroad, stay easily with me in my mind and many memories happily bob to its surface.

On leaving the Navy I had returned to my job on a provincial newspaper where it soon became clear to those who knew me that I would not be staying there for long.

Thinking back now it would seem that there had been an inevitability to every step that I had taken but that had not been the case when I was falteringly taking them. From the age of sixteen or so my ambition to be the editor of *Picture Post* or *Life* magazine or *Paris Match* had resolved itself into a nameless urge unreasonably prompting me to regard all that I did or heard or read or saw as preparation for an existence which I had been quite unable to define. Its more crass manifestation perhaps lay in my unspoken wish not to be a chronicler and photographer of persons and events, a task for which my newspaper was carefully tutoring me, but to become the person at the heart of the events which were being chronicled and photographed. It had been while pondering thus, I fancy, that O'Liver and I had first collided.

An old newspaper sweat, just come from a coroner's inquest on a young woman who had been murdered, was with relish reciting details of what he had heard and seen to a few sitting in the press room of a town hall, when I had entered, sent there on an errand by my boss, the art editor.

'This should interest a randy little bastard like you,' the sweat had said grinning nastily at me. 'The killer had bitten off the nipples from both her tits.'

This young trainee journalist and photographer, then in the summer of his seventeenth year, had not been able to cope adequately with this disquieting information; had, in fact, felt more sick than his hard-acquired, tough Hunsbeckian patina would have allowed him to show. Feigning indifference, I had lit up a twopenny Woodbine, given counsel on the result of the 2.30, turned up my raincoat collar, left the press room and had headed away to the nearest pub I hoped would serve me. Not being eighteen, the age at which the law allowed one to consume alcohol on the premises, had been an obstacle over which I used to hop by being tall, wearing my mac, smoking thoughtfully, studying a newspaper and, crowning touch, screwing on my head a flat, cloth cap that I used to keep about my person for the specific purpose of upping up my age a couple of years. It didn't always work but it was worth a try and, anyway, what could they do, shoot me?

Fitting on my headpiece, willing myself to be at least eighteen, I had been about to enter the boozer when, gangling along from the opposite direction, I saw a tall young man, obviously thirsty, stuffing into his back pocket a cap distinctively striped with the colours of a local public school and who fired at me a defiantly quizzical glance. Being eighteen is a serious business for a sixteen-year-old, so we had paid each other no further heed, had gone into the bar where, lowering my voice to a more manful register, I ordered a pint of plain, listened to this schoolboy baritoning for the same, passed a disagreeable moment until my request was accepted, paid, and then had sunk my face into the froth and drunk deeply down. On emerging, it became clear that the schoolboy, too, had got away with it, for there he stood busily sucking his juice and lighting up a fag.

My mind had been disturbed by murderers and mutilated women but now shone clean of such torments, purged by a mouthful of bitter ale swallowed in the company of a delinquent fellow spirit.

Some months later my boss took the unusual step of inviting me out for morning coffee to a café round the corner where the bigger wigs of the newspaper world used to gather. There he told me that a friend and colleague of his, a distinguished figure on the staff of a national newspaper, had a son who was precociously gifted, intelligent, charming, but a touch unruly, wayward, rebellious. Perhaps, thought my boss, it might be an idea for me to meet this young chap because, my boss continued to think, the boy resembled me in manner, speech, even in appearance and that there might, might mind you, might be common ground for the pair of us to share and to that end, my boss finally thought, he would arrange for us two to meet.

In a little short while we did meet, O'Liver and I; met again, chortled of caps, licensing laws and the pub, chattered of this, contradicted each other of that, informed each other of such, reassured each other of the like, pinned our ears back and snarled, made ourselves plain about one thing, agreed that t'other was uncertain, I knew a bank whereon the wild thyme blows, he knew that all was foul and fit to screech in, my soul was an old horse offered for sale in twenty fairs, his chosen comrades thought at school he must grow into a famous man; our hurly-burly friendship was begun that day, it is far from over yet.

Later, at his home, having been introduced to his parents, his tall, grave father, studious, welcoming, kind; his mother, lithe, quick, attractive, mischievous, I was standing staring at a painting by Martin Froy as through the room moved a poet a painter an academic and a writer, all with their sophisticated women, my big tongue unusually knotted, my feelings in such company bottled, my mind scrabbling together sensible sentences should anyone speak to me of anything at all, when O'Liver's mother came

77

up to me. She looked at me, smiled, and then quietly intoned in my ear:

'There was a young woman called Rhoda
Who kept an illicit pagoda
Whose halls and whose walls
Were festooned with the balls
And the tools of the fools who bestrode her.'

A dozen or so years ago, shortly after his mother had died, O'Liver and I sat in his cottage out there among the Yorkshire dales and he quietly grieved for her as we talked. He had found his mum's funeral service to be a trying business, some of the tears shed had been real and he honoured those but the words that had been spoken there by strangers, well, if not exactly bogus, had not been, how should he put it, a true reflection of his impish old mum's larky shade, had lacked, perhaps, a quality to be found only in her cherished, salty limericks, a form of ode not included in the requiems of English Protestantism, an omission that we should both immediately and in a secular manner rectify.

From the cottage to the pub and when the barrels all were empty from the pub to the cottage, solo, duet and in chorus, sobbing noisily, we scavenged our slaughtered brains and throughout that northern night had hymned O'Liver's dead mother with the young man from Australia right to Rhoda's pagoda. Before he tumbled into bed and soft oblivion, O'Liver had asked that, in the case of his dying before me, would I see to it that at his funeral jazzmen play 'We Shall Walk Through The Streets Of The City'?

I shall, O'Liver, I shall. Also shall I drink hot gin and piss in your grave.

ALL THROUGH the hours and the days, the months and the years that followed upon my meeting with O'Liver, the threads and strands, patches and nothings of all my doings collected themselves into the mortal fabric which is imperfect me. No one, the good the bad or the loathsome mediocrities, has had on me a greater or more timely influence than O'Liver.

We both are old now, more sedate, more responsible, we sleep in beds and sometimes we are sober; our bones are brittle, our sinews want elastic, the optician is kept busy and the dentist's in despair, the barber gives us shorter shrift while the tailor makes thick overcoats, but should a shining occasion present itself, why, we will run jump fight fuck wheel a barrow drive a truck and generally present ourselves, singly or in tandem, to whatever merry mayhem takes our fancy. So had it been when I hung up my old hat, stepped out of my bell-bottoms, pulled on my civilian strides and returned to work on the newspaper.

WHICH OF us had had the idea of becoming involved with that Arts Centre I no longer know but involved we both became. Perhaps it was me, there had, after all, been a small theatre on its blessed top and access to a Civic Theatre which had staged early productions of Synge and Chekhov, that and my own emerging propensities for matters theatrical. Perhaps it had been O'Liver, for the lovely middle of the building housed potters, painters, encouraged poets and poetry and had been visited by Jacob Kramer and John Heath Stubbs. Perhaps the pair of us had fallen in there together, for at its dingy bottom the building hosted the Marxist Association and the Young Communist League, glum sods indeed who we might have felt needed cheering up by claiming our deathless allegiance to Anarchism, Fascism or Syndicalism, none of which notions we had cleaved to at all but it was great gas conjuring up spectres of Bakunin, D'Annunzio and Larkin. Maybe one of our two pairs of sensitive nostrils had scented the whiff of women, sandwiches, comparative wealth, tolerance and beer. No matter, whatever one of us avers the other will flatly contradict thus producing a little spark, but shortly after my demobilisation a lot of my interest lived gainfully in that building while less and less of it prospered at my newspaper. An intolerable situation, one that was grossly unfair to my employers, to the very ethos of that establishment which had given me so much, so much, and which had asked in return only that I do my best, which I was palpably not doing.

That situation could not and did not continue.

O'Liver had been indifferently attending a college of art but was beginning to paint startlingly well, not in the manner of his vividly coloured abstractions which three or four years later were to win him praise and prizes at London, but figures and portraits, in his own way conservative and traditional, hued in haunting greys and greens and blues. My lamentable efforts at short plays and long poems were becoming increasingly dreary. One in particular getting deserved hoots had been an Arthurian borrowing based on a photograph taken at the funeral of King George VI showing the Queen, the Queen Mother and the dowager Queen Mother, veiled in black. The eloquence of this testimony to the mourning of a royal house had bulged large in my mind, had reminded me of the three queens, shrouded, mysterious, sailing in to bear off the body of Arthur and unfortunately had prompted me to scrawl down a feeble, halting version of this event as observed not only by Bedevere but also by post-war, angry young me. Its brightest moment came when it, too, had hit the fire.

Christmas was coming, the Centre annually staged a celebratory romp and I had been willingly roped in to perform in it, playing Idle Jack or some such. The show had come, been a giggle, and gone when, shortly after, a Mr Awad asked could he have a private word with me. Certainly.

Awad was actively preparing a stage adaptation of Turgenev's *Fathers and Sons*, dates for its performance at the Civic Theatre were set, the principle roles of Anna and Bazarov were to be played by professionals but the leading man was ill and Awad, Turkish but reared in Yorkshire, asked me if I would take over.

It was only reasonable to point out to Sultan Ben Awad that my performance in the Christmas show had been only the second time in my life that I had appeared on stage, the first being a performance committed three or so years earlier when I had played a rum-swigging uncommunicative sea captain called Red Molloy in an amateur production of *Aloma of the South Seas*. This play had been presented by an institution for whom I was then playing rugby. My involvement, and that of half the rugger team, had been as makeweight to a large cast, and we had shared the eventually realised hope of bumping about among rings of writhing, browned-up maidens, wreathed in *leis*, bare-breasted, who, to harmonies of ukelele and ocharina, swayed around in sarongs.

Awad had patiently listened to my chunter before surprising me by saying that the few minutes he had seen me on stage during the Christmas frolic had persuaded him that I had the makings of becoming an actor. He had then given me the script, suggested that I seriously considered playing the part of Bazarov, asked me to be kind enough to let him know my answer, yes or no, by the end of the week and had left me alone to brood on this and on a great deal more.

Up to that time my mind had allowed itself to ruminate no further than on a vague wish to be in some way involved with a working theatre, maybe to find work which would allow me to learn production or administration or stage management. Dreams only, images and whispers in a young man's brain, a twenty-year-old sure only of a dissatisfaction with his chosen job and an uncertain future.

A regular cinema-goer, an occasional theatregoer, of course I had considered being an actor, but as to any practical moves to see whether I could or could not act I had made none at all. To be sure, the notion was contained in my great scheme of being poet and playwright, occasionally appearing in performances of my own work for the theatre and the cinema, but my poetry was pitiful, my plays untroubled by being uttered onto paper and the only performance of any length or substance that I had given had been, for two years, the not entirely convincing one of he who goes down to the sea in ships.

At almost forty years' remove it is an easy business for me to say that the play Awad had given me to read was no more than a trivial attempt to make one of the themes of a Turgenev novel into a romantic, popular offering to an audience, but at that time, having not read the book, wrapped in glad ignorance, I had read the play, found it likeable, found the character Bazarov to be a lively bloke, one who, if not exactly a man to go hunting tigers with, then surely one to share a blather, crack a bottle or steal a woman from.

I decided to do it, let that be known and then for the first time in my life had got stuck into the toils of studying a part for performance. A true amateur dilettante, I had learned the part, startled bus queues as I passed by bursting into bits of it, alarmed colleagues on the newspaper who discovered me in corridors bitterly raving at no one at all, while at rehearsals I had been awkward, self-conscious and desperately unsure of myself. Awad had calmed me; Awad had helped, joking me into confidence and self-assurance.

The play had opened, was well received, well attended, pronounced successful and I became the subject of a buzz of attention which had reassuringly not all been kind.

A few nights after its close I had walked into the Arts Centre and heard a poignant and unusual air being played on the piano there. A peep into the room showed me the pianist: a man who sat with an upright posture, at whiles his head tilted back, at whiles tilting forward, seeming to examine the keys as gracefully he played. Quietly, in a pure, tenor voice, he began to sing; he sang words which I knew but couldn't precisely locate, familiar words, all right, but words heard, read or spoken in a different context as through my density at last they penetrated. It was Eliot's 'The Journey of the Magi'.

After a time, seemingly dissatisfied, he stopped playing. I said hello, he said hello, I told of my astonishment at hearing the poem sung, he told me with a bubbling chuckle that he'd seen me in the play and began rapping on the piano again, I asked him did he mind if I listened, he answered that he didn't give a toss if I broke into a tap dance but if I would cock an ear I might hear something interesting. I had cocked an ear and listened as he played and sang lyrics by Shakespeare set to music composed by Warlock, a man whose name I knew but whose work I had not before heard. Listening, I had watched him with real interest, a poised man whose panache and skill admitted no effort as he played, as he sang, as he tilted back his head, as he smoothly leaned forward, his profile nobly severe, his manner confident, his control and his care of the music keen, and as he finished his playing with a rippling flourish, he pulled his hands up from the keys to hold them still below his face, gazing down with a quiet smile as his music faded.

Phillip Stone it was, now my distinguished colleague and easy friend, then a man, previously unknown to me, racked by tuberculosis who had been ten years earlier a gifted and successful young actor in London. Year after coughing bloody year after year had Mr Phillip Stone struggled to survive in hospital after hospital, battling to be once again a fit and able man and actor. Physically depleted, that time when we had first met, his spirit was strong and his determination to rejoin the profession that he knew so well and loved so much would be realised three years later when, in a play by Sacha Guitry, once again, he began excellently to practise it.

'Do you think you're an actor?' had said this unknown warbling pianist to me, unchallenging eyes smiling, a calm authority in his manner.

Well, not really, of course, but, what with having thought a bit about it, having, as it were, leanings, inner nudgings, having just knocked them dead in an amateur production of an unknown play in a comparatively little heard of theatre in a suburb of this city in the northern part of England, it had crossed my mind that, all things being equal, if I could pick up a tip or two, that is, on how to set about it, or, for that matter, how to set about setting about it, why, well then, perhaps I might give it a stab.

Phillip had heard of our establishment, of its mix and mingle of artists of all sorts, mostly amateur, some professional, and had been invited to give his views on the production in which I had recently glittered. This he had done, had not spared us but neither had he been patronising or cruel as, from notes made during a performance, he had put a penetrating intelligence on our offering: acting, staging, scenery, lighting, costumes, music. On the wincing subject of me he had been wickedly funny, alarmingly perceptive and, though I had been left unbutchered, his implications were clear: I was a presumptuous prat who had a great deal to learn.

After his talk, Phillip had stepped onto the stage of the little attic theatre, sat on a chair and, lit by the light from a table lamp, had performed, hauntingly, Pirandello's dramatic monologue, *The Man with a Flower in his Mouth.*

True, Mr Stone, there was a great deal ahead of me to do; but he knew and I knew that I was stumblingly about to start doing it. Requests for the prospectuses of various drama schools were penned off, received, mulled over, their common denominator turning out to be how much such training would cost; an unexpected invitation to meet the producer of a local repertory company gladdened me, was accepted, turned out to be a chat about my inexperience, was not discouraging, and left me where it found me; evening tutoring by a scrumptious former actress was in its turn assuredly instructive but perhaps not wholly pertinent to my immediate practical needs; a diet of books on drama, plays and theatrical biography became my daily fare; the newspaper and I wished each other God speed and we made our dry-eyed farewells; I doffed my natty suit and, to gather a bundle of the folding green lettuce, donned blue overalls and set out, off and up to be a demolition man and steeplejack.

Clambering and hammering through the day let weekends and the nights run free for me to practise theatre, trying my hand at much: movement, singing, acting, audition pieces, scenery and staging a one-act play.

The play, of course, had needed a set; for this job, naturally, there had been no better man than O'Liver; free drink, women and a promise of sandwiches led him into the attic theatre; there he had drawn and glued and built and painted.

The night before the kick off, during the fitting up of the set and the lighting, O'Liver had pronounced himself dissatisfied with a fair portion of his work; had then cast out what offended his eye by kicking it down into bits, thus providing us with an opportunity to find a radical solution for this problem sharpish. 'What is needed,' he had eventually said, 'is about one hundred brick-shaped objects.'

A short stroll only had taken us to a spot where there was a proliferation of such fine things, with an unemployed wheelbarrow resting near. That had proved handy; through the night we gathered and transported our raw material and, after having walked the wheelbarrow home, by dawn we were painting all the fucking brick-shaped objects white.

Did you ever use a drawer from a chest of them as a hod? If you have then you will know that when it's your turn for the side with the two little handles, it is wise to ensure they are firmly fixed into their station. Failure to do this can mean that after numerous and laborious trips up three flights of stairs lugging your loaded hod, one of the little handles comes off in your grasp and the whole load tips heavily onto your and your assistant's poor feet.

The play had been well acted, well received, and O'Liver's set, a daisy.

In the attic of a building by a little-known theatre, in a suburb of a city in the northern part of England, some there considered me to be hot stuff.

TIME TO move, now. Time to don rucksacks, to point directive thumbs, to aim in the general direction of London.

A wedge of wages in our pockets, mine got by swaying about on the tops of brewery chimneys, O'Liver's jingle provided perhaps by burglary, certainly by threats, a lorry heading for Birmingham had kindly allowed us to bump along with it on its weathered, unloaded back. After our arrival there we had shared in a pub a feast of hard-boiled eggs and beer with the driver, then we set off by foot or by thumb for near enough Stratford-upon-Avon; Michael Redgrave was playing King Lear there. Warm days, mild nights, we had kipped not uncomfortably in a bus station; an early start in the queue for tickets at the box office had realised us two good seats for the evening's performance; we were elected. The house and shop where Shakespeare was born and where he had lived from infancy to young manhood, and his tomb, stay with me from that time; they made him seem only mortal.

As we tourists, O'Liver and I, trundled down by the riverside, a swan, pounding its weighty wings powerfully into the water, took off to straight-fly a hundred yards or so; the scale and strength of the long-necked black-headed bird, so beautiful, so brutal, so huge and deadly the wide white wings, had surprised me and impressed me and had prompted me to consider that swans are very large dickie birds indeed and are in no way lightly to be trifled with. A consideration which turned out to be correct when, practically a decade later, sailing on the lightless river Avon in stolen punts, my companions and I encountered a baleful horde of them.

Good mates, all companions from the company playing at the Biscuit Factory, Memorial Theatre, all cheerful, tired, most not sad that the long season was ending, all glad it had been a good one, we had chosen that dark time before daybreak to go punting along the river, seeking for to pay a call upon the morning swans.

The punt I captained had on its pole, Whynot, P., former

sailor, muttering much of port, starboard, midships and helm as we floundered around in the reeds and the mud. Spotty Dotty was skipper of the other punt, on her pole swayed Old Scout singing, agonised, of how he had shot his own Molly Bawn, miraculously staying on board as he stuffed his pole down hard, ramming the punt in circles.

Sprawled around drinking from bottles, our crews kept watch.

First light soon brought warming sun; navigation and poles-manship brought us to the river's middle; gently rotating there, we rode in line abreast.

A great flock of swans, rough-necked, rude, their eyes filled with murder, rose as one and savagely flew at us in a great white beating fury. All of us bar Spotty Dotty hit the dip. All of us. None bar Spotty Dotty was spared a trip into the wetness. None. Our lives spared thus, *Twelfth Night*, *The Taming of the Shrew*, *The Merchant of Venice*, *Troilus and Cressida*, we heaved about the river, nor wondered how Spotty Dotty had stayed dry.

THE WINDOWS of the dressing rooms at the back of the Stratford Memorial Theatre face over the river bank; there had I stood awhile an hour or so before curtain up on *King Lear*, glimpsing figures through the glass and the opened frames, had then walked through the foyer, sat in the packed auditorium; the lights dimmed, the play began.

Bustling, gruff, vigorous and ancient, Michael Redgrave's Lear came pounding onto the stage, a king; a warrior; a huge dangerous man whose absolute authority lived as much in his personality and physique as in any inherited sovereignty, one for whom dissent might provoke a reach for the nearest battleaxe and a summary removal of the dissenter from his head. Preoccupied, rash, a touch gaga, his command to Gloucester that he attend the noble suitors of Cordelia held long familiarity with the Duke, irritation at his

87

possible neglect of duty in this regard and a royal awareness of niceties and the protocols binding the rituals of his court; the deep centre of this aristocratic, iron age, ruling warrior élite.

Lowering over all in the setting was a great stone monolith, while stout timber, bronze, gold, luxurious cloth and sharp hacking weaponry suggested a legendary ancient Britain in a time before Merlin, before chivalry, before Christ; the time in which Shakespeare sets his mighty version of this old European myth of Lear and his daughters.

The last couple of decades have served up to us some productions of this play in which Lear has been performed as a peevish old prat who deserves all he gets from his daughters, Regan and Goneril. Why poor bloody Shakespeare and his faithful audiences should be visited by these distortions and latterday Nahum Tatery is a painful puzzlement to me. No one in Shakespeare's *Lear* gets what they deserve. There is no justice, human or providential, in the play; there is no redemption; for three hours we share Shakespeare's unflinching gaze at the extreme nature of man's estate, within and without, human and cosmic, the condition and predicament of humankind where fine notions of love, duty, authority, charity, loyalty, humanity, pity, kindness, bravery, even of simple goodness are ripped and split by human malignity and the godless accidents of time and circumstance and we see ourselves to be no more in nature than a 'bare, forked radish'.

In the late seventeenth century, after the restoration of the monarchy and the playhouse, maybe there had been a sickly need to let Nahum Tate loose on *King Lear* and rewrite Shakespeare, thus providing romance, sentimentality and a happy ending to audiences who, so I am told, yearned to be virtuously uplifted. Maybe, indeed; but events of the subsequent centuries shatteringly demonstrate that such tinkering didn't do the delicate sensibilities of many much lasting good, and in our period, after Auschwitz, to perform the play in a way that provides any character with a dainty justification for his or her actions is perversely silly.

Daddy 1910. Ireland.

Whatever, I cavil; Edmund Kean it was who, in the early eighteen hundreds, restored Shakespeare's text. It is recorded that that great actor pointed at Shakespeare's play, at the last soul-racking scene and said, 'That is the sacred page I am yet to expound. The London audience have no notion of what I can do until they see me over the dead body of Cordelia.' Kean. London and cities around the world soon had a notion of what that ferocious little imp could do, both on and off the stage. A bit of a scamp he was, our Edmund. The biographies, pictures and anecdotes of Kean, John Barrymore and Henry Irving owned the matter which gripped me more tightly than that of any other actor in those days when I was twenty and wondering if I could or would or dared emulate them.

One yarn about Kean continues to produce a chuckle from me. Prior to a performance of *Richard the Third*, Kean and his great mate Cooke had been on the piss. Kean was to give his Richard and Cooke his Buckingham, both, in the written words of the stage manager at the time, were 'very wide'. When uttering Crookback's soliloquy, 'Now is the winter of our discontent/Made glorious summer by this son of York', Kean, it seems, was having a little difficulty with his diction. Someone in the audience, evidently disapproving of such irresponsible slurring of the dickie birds, words, loudly suggested that Mr Kean was drunk. Kean accepted this information, looked into the wings where Cooke in an attempt to remain upright was draped around the prompter, looked back in the general direction of the audience and said: 'If you think I'm drunk wait till you see the Duke of Buckingham.'

One time during the splendid and ridiculous sixties, we were filming through a Paris night, close by the chilly river Seine, with the small hours near, when an actress and I had to perform a short scene. The entire unit was sensibly muffled up against the nip. I was wearing long underwear beneath my suit and, having no lines to speak, had insulated myself with a drop of brandy and soda. Not so the graceful and talented young beauty with whom

I was to play the scene. Spiffingly decked in high fashion, right enough, but not proof against the bitter chill. 'If only to be warm were gorgeous'. *Lear*. Thus flimsily bedight the girl had in the scene to exit a building, walk down a flight of stairs, approach where I was sitting in the passenger seat of an open roadster sports car, say a line, hop into the driver's seat, say another line, start the car and then drive rapidly off.

Un morceau de gateau.

Alas, the shrewd bite of the cold had penetrated through the frail wrappings round my fair friend the actress, had stiffened quite her bones and had turned the lovely girl bright blue.

Blue as certain cheeses.

The cameraman had a concerned chunter with the director. It seemed to me that the answer might lie in taking the lady into my caravan and tossing down her dainty throat a fair slug of brandy, which, of course, I did. The roses immediately bloomed in her cheeks, light shone in her dove's eyes and a glow replaced the chilled chatter in her. Vivacious, warm and ready to go we returned to play our parts.

Lights were lit, camera turning, director said, 'Action', and down the stairs lightly skipped my leading lady, came to the car, expertly played her lines, sprang into the seat, talked, switched on the ignition, put her into gear, pressed the accelerator and away we shot like a fucking rocket. Nor was our whizzing impeded by the huge tripods bearing big carbon arc lamps, or the lamplighters up there trimming them. All came thundering down as we zoomed right through the clattering pylons. No one was hurt, there were banter and chuckles and the scene turned out to be a dilly. Later, I told my sweet colleague the story of Kean and Cooke.

At the end of filming the lady gave me for a keepsake a beautifully bound copy of Milton's *Paradise Lost*. It lives in my study. I've just had a peep at it. It is signed 'The Duke of Buckingham'.

IN THE year when I was twenty, a year of bumming and moiling and seeking, I also saw Donald Wolfit play Lear; he gave a famously volcanic and profoundly moving performance.

That night, though, at Stratford, sitting with O'Liver in the audience, Michael Redgrave and the whole cast and production made it seem to me that I had received the play entirely.

After the curtain, O'Liver and I found a tidy pub where over a pint of beer my old china happily indulged me and my marvelling at the modernity and naturalness of much of the play's language. O'Liver agreed with my enthusiasms and further added that, in his view, the play defined true madness.

'Send for Dick Surgeon, I'm cut to the brains.'

Then, after having instructed me in the geographical and historical implications of the set, plus where we would find its like in Cornwall even now, we addressed ourselves to snore. We decided as the night was warm and dry that we would kip in the hay baled safely in a field that we had spotted. And so we did. Snug as bugs in rugs we were when we curled up in a hollow of the big bales of hay. It seemed, however, wise to us both that, against a possible onset of cold snap when snoozing, it were better if we sprinkled over ourselves some of this here hay stuff. We dug deeply into the bales for armsful of crinkling warm provender. The more we got, it was so warm yet fragile, the more we wanted, so deeply down we dug and dug eventually to discover that all the fine hay was merely the cosy cover to great square chunks of fertilising shit. Hot shit.

There were no swans and no one near us on the following morning when we dipped our feet and faces into the River Avon, in preparation for our assault on London.

Shit. Did you ever find yourself in the dark up to your shoulders in hot shit?

The roll to London that we thumbed proved a lark. The only room not reserved on the metropolis-bound lorry was a dodgy perch, standing on top of empty beer barrels clunking and skidding about on the open back of the vehicle. Eventually we safely arrived at London, thankfully pitched ourselves off the barrelling lorry at Euston station and headed for the men's hostel where we had booked rooms and which stood by the Tottenham Court Road.

We had not slept well, our rest had been fitful, malodorous, not to be recommended and so we were purposefully trudging towards a bath, grub, a change of gear and perhaps a quiet kip when we happened on a door centred in a carved white stone surround.

Sculpted above the door on the left stood a lightsome lass effortlessly balancing above her pretty head a boulder, which scrutiny revealed to be a representation in rock of Melpomene, the muse of tragedy. On the right, his stockings falling down, stood a neurotic fat boy heaving above his nut the muse of comedy, Thalia. Above the door was carved 'The Royal Academy of Dramatic Art'.

This possible gateway to my future had unexpectedly loomed up only a hundred yards or so along from the spot where we had tumbled off the lorry and was minutes only away from the men's hostel. It therefore seemed to me to be only right and timely that I should immediately pop into the premises and give them a thorough casing. Sensing my intention, O'Liver pointed out that our choice of lodgings the previous evening had left me not fragrant but that if I was so minded he would, in the anticipation that I would be shortly hosed from the building by a person with a clothes peg on his nose, wait for me outside.

A cool marble entrance hall met me as I wandered in there, a corridor ran across an elegant branching stairway ahead of me, at its base stood a bronze head of my adored Bernard Shaw. There was activity, too, as well-dressed men and women, young, mature or elderly moved hither and yon, some speaking in quiet well-enunciated voices, others silent, thoughtful, all generating a sense of excitement, intense yet serene. Bernard Shaw drew me to him. I gazed at him for quite a while, finding the sculpture enchanting, all whiskers and wisdom and Lucifer, human, comedic and brave.

A voice behind me told me that it was by Epstein. I turned to find the voice wearing the uniform of a military sergeant: dark blue, three golden stripes, capped, buttoned, smart and brightly shining. Inside the uniform was Sergeant, tall, slim, no longer young, lively, stern and friendly. He told me that Shaw had been the academy's most active patron, that, until his death some two years before, Shaw had often been a visitor there, invariably bringing with him good humour and good sense.

I told Sergeant the story of the dimwit beauty who had suggested to Shaw that they produce a child, that with her looks and Shaw's brains they would give the world a rare infant, how Shaw had declined the suggestion, stating that if the babe was born with her brains and his looks they might give the world a rare cretin.

Sergeant found this funny so I told him of the exchange of telegrams between Shaw and Churchill.

Shaw: FIRST NIGHT OF MY PLAY NEXT WEEK STOP   TICKETS RESERVED STOP   BRING FRIEND IF YOU HAVE ONE.
Churchill: UNABLE TO MAKE FIRST NIGHT STOP   WILL COME SECOND NIGHT STOP   IF THERE IS ONE.

This, too, amused Sergeant and I do believe he was about to lay one of his stock of Shavian anecdotes on me when we were interrupted by a tall, burly, distinguished elderly gentleman eager to know the cause of our mirth. Sergeant stood to attention; I thought it appropriate to tell of my admiration for the sculpture, how Sergeant had identified the sculptor for me and how this had led me into a couple of yarns about the artist's subject.

The distinguished gentleman asked me to repeat them to him. This I did. He had heard them before but still he smiled, smiled and then told me of how one time he had been up all night with Shaw, attending a difficult dress rehearsal of one of his plays. How he and the septuagenarian GBS had emerged from the theatre just before dawn, how Shaw had refused an offer to find him a taxi saying that as he lived only a couple of miles away he should prefer to run, which he had done. White hair and whiskers streaming, legs knickerbockered and stockinged, he had galloped away down the deserted St Martin's Lane.

Sergeant marched away to his post at the neat small guardroom by the entrance and I was left to continue my conversation with this brusquely affable, elderly gentleman who, I was soon to learn, turned out to be Sir Kenneth Barnes, Principal of the RADA.

What precisely we said I can no longer recall. Something about his wondering if I was a student and my replying that technically I was not but assuredly was hopeful of becoming one. Of forms, we talked, and of filling them in; of interviews, granted or denied, of correspondence entered into and despatched to and fro, of auditions for entrance, of their importance, of how these important auditions for the coming autumn term were being held that week, how candidates for these important auditions were chosen from forms filled, correspondence written, interviews satisfactorily concluded.

One wondered aloud, I fancy, that though it was not to be doubted that these usual channels needs must be gone through, might not there, perhaps, be an odd occasion when chance, circumstance, presence on the spot, voyages on black northern seas, time and tide, good will and good faith could conjoin, thus obviating these normally necessary preliminaries?

Sir Kenneth looked at Bernard Shaw, then at me, and then at his watch. I looked at my watch, 2 p.m., then at Bernard Shaw, and then at Sir Kenneth.

'Be at my office at four forty-five this afternoon,' said Sir Kenneth.

I said, 'Thank you, sir.'

Bernard Shaw looked on.

Outside, leaning against Melpomene, O'Liver was smoking thoughtfully. 'Some interesting customers coming in and going out of this shop,' he said. 'Did you get your shitty foot in the door?' A nod from me and then off we trotted to the hostel.

At the reception a note was handed to me. It was from the hostel secretary, a man I'd played rugger against a couple of times. It said that he was in his office should I need anything and did I remember the time in Manchester when Frank the Law had had half his ear chopped off?

It was nice to see him again, interesting to remark that he was approximately my size and shape and delightful to see that he was smartly dressed in a navy blue blazer and dark grey trousers. A narrow corridor letting into half a dozen or so single bedrooms was our accommodation, with a communal bath and lavatory room at one end. Within minutes I was stewing in a soapy tub where it slowly occurred to me that in no way was I at all nervous. Later, shaving carefully, I watched in the mirror as O'Liver sleepily shuffled through the bathroom to bolt himself into one of the cubicles housing a lavatory there. 'Ta ta, Flyblown, see you later,' I called into O'Liver's booth.

'Good luck,' he grunted as I, spruce, nay, natty in the secretary's jacket and trousers, set off out of the hostel, walked down to and around the University of London, lingered for a while in a leafy park nearby there and then headed for the RADA, arriving there at four thirty on the dot.

My spontaneously arranged interview with Sir Kenneth seems to me to have lasted only minutes. He had bowled me a lifter by first asking what I considered to be my weaknesses. He had then sat back in the chair at his desk and regarded me seated opposite him as I mustered my reply.

Resisting any temptation to present him with choice examples from my hefty catalogue of frailties, I had made as if my understanding of his question referred only to matters theatrical and answered his question with a reference to my inexperience, my understanding that an actor's art took many long years to learn, that shortly before his death Henry Irving had said to Bram Stoker that for one who had begun his acting life not being able to talk or move very well he hadn't done too badly, Irving had said, and what a pity, now he was just getting the hang of it, that soon it would have to end.

Sir Kenneth asked me what I knew of Irving. Only what I'd read, I told him, and heard, and of the many photographs and portraits of him that I had seen, of my estimation that a man who had staged and performed so many plays so successfully for thirty years must have been extraordinary indeed.

'He was,' said Sir Kenneth. 'He was an extraordinary man. He was a great actor. I saw him act. I saw him when I was quite young. He had exceptional power. He could be frighteningly sinister and menacing but his chief virtue as an actor was his simplicity. He didn't use greasepaint, you know, he preferred watercolour.'

My portion on this earth seemed to take on another dimension. Here was I seated opposite a man who had seen and had met Irving. Here was theatre and history and experience palpably seated opposite me talking affably of what were, to me, legends and far-off mysteries only. He spoke of Irving as I might of Steve Donahue the jockey. 'Your personal weaknesses, I mean,' said Sir Kenneth, yanking me back to cases, his strong mind rat-trapping me on his original point.

What I had chuntered out to him escapes me now. It had probably been no more than a muted litany of resistible temptations which would have served well enough coming from the mouth of any young man not too keen to confide his predilections for whiskey, women, gambling, jazz, japes, larks and riotous assembly. Whatever I may have burbled out, I finished by telling Sir Kenneth that, whatever my weaknesses might be, something told me that I would be able to cope with the knocks that the profession dishes out

as part of an actor's daily lot, that a statement made by Edmund
Kean to his son Charles had given me pause and thought and
determination.

Sir Kenneth asked me what Kean had said.

Charles Kean, I answered him, after an education at Eton and
Oxford, one night told his father that he intended to become an
actor. Kean had listened gravely to his son, paused, nodded, and
had then said, 'Can you starve, Cocky?'

Sir Kenneth hadn't heard that before, but he seemed to like it,
yes, he liked it, he must remember that, yes, the profession could be
very cruel, yes, Sybil said one needed the skin of a rhinoceros and
the heart of a tiger, yes, that, perhaps, was overstating it, yes, but
he quite liked what Kean had said, yes, he must remember that.

'Can you starve, Cocky?'

An abrupt change in his manner followed on this musing as,
busily and with a seeming spasm of irritation, he began shuffling
through papers on his desk while asking me if I wished to be a
student at the RADA.

Yes.

Was I aware that one auditioned for entrance before a panel
of judges? That if chosen to be one of the 10 per cent selected by
the examiners as a possible candidate for study, that there would
be a further examination at a later date when that first 10 per cent
would be reduced to 3 per cent. That quite often there was a third
audition, that if, however, one had progressed to that stage but
did not succeed in gaining entrance, the unlucky candidates were
usually recommended to the Preparatory Academy to the Royal
Academy of Dramatic Art for one year's course of study. That the
fees were payable in advance, that there were some scholarships
which were awarded by the RADA and some few others granted
by local education committees if the candidate were to be strongly
recommended by the examining judges as fitting to receive one.

'You are, of course, fully prepared to give an audition,' growled
the now grumpy Principal of the Royal Academy of Dramatic Art.

'Of course.'

'Here are the required set pieces,' he said, handing me an impressive two-page document. 'A candidate must audition with one of the speeches that we have listed as well as material of his own choosing. We shall see you at ten thirty a.m. on Friday.'

This last had been wholly unexpected. The most I had hoped for was to bypass months that the slapping about of letters and literature would have occupied. Friday? The day after next?

Disbelief can provide a numbness which tides one over very nicely until reality rubs it quite away. By the time I had bidden *au revoir* to the Principal, was heading, as instructed, for the registrar and the secretary to have my particulars taken, the fact of Friday, of an audition to be given in less than two days, of a real chance to become a drama student, had set my mental meter ticking and made my mouth dry as cork.

At some point during my blithely croaked assurances to an important person that the fees were no deterrent to my enrolment at the academy and the giving of my personal details to another, I had copped a squint at the two pages of speeches handed to me by Sir Kenneth, one of which had to be performed at my audition on Friday. Bang in the middle of the second page there was a family favourite: Higgins to Eliza from the second act of Bernard Shaw's *Pygmalion*. 'You are to live here for the next six months learning how to speak beautifully like a lady in a florist's shop.'

At the beginning of the war my mother had taken me to see the film version any number of times, subsequently I had chewed the play often, had memorised chunks of it and, more, the matter of this particular speech was common currency between my mother, father, sister and myself. If one of us was rumbled when committing a perceived wrong, another would often weigh in with, 'You will be taken to the Tower of London where your head will be cut off as a warning to other presumptuous flower girls': if another's actions seemed to shine with goodness, one of us might readily pipe up, 'You shall have lots to eat and money to buy chocolates and take rides in taxis.'

Under the stairway at the RADA my bronze friend with the green patina was playing a blinder.

Calm came to me, hushing away anxieties and uncertainty. Go over the speech time and time again tonight and tomorrow. Give a similar thrashing to 'O, what a rogue and peasant slave am I', *Hamlet*, Shakespeare, a piece already polished, and, come Friday, breathe deeply and then go for broke. Thus, tranquil and confident, I prepared to depart this academy which had already proved surprisingly kind to me.

Sergeant was standing in the hall, once more I directed his gaze to the sculpture of Shaw. On my way to join the navy, I told him, when rattling about on a railway train, I had read in a newspaper of Shaw's death. The report had also stated that after breaking yet another bone some days earlier, Shaw had said, 'If I survive this, I shall be immortal.'

'He was immortal well before he died,' said Sergeant cryptically. It would have been graceless, surely, to have disagreed.

———————

BACK IN the bathroom at the hostel, happily replacing the secretary's feathers with my own less gorgeous gear, plucked from its rucksack, the sounds of groans and discomfort came sighing to me from one of the lavatory cubicles. A bolt snapped open and from the very spot that I had earlier seen him enter, an unhappy O'Liver, dead-legged, stooped, stricken and cursing, came shuffle shuffle from the booth in which for two hours and more he had been sleeping astride the porcelain.

The needling ache of circulation restored giving the deadened parts of him severe gyp, his face an old crumpled newspaper telling of agony and dismay, oaths whinnying out of him, he commenced a little prance on the spot, a little shaking of the numbed arms, a little attempt to unknot the bowline of his frame.

At that point, keen to have a wee-wee, a fellow resident entered and was perhaps surprised to find a naked me delighted at the plight of an animated scarecrow. He stuck himself in the appropriate stall, relieved himself, and then, when rapidly departing the scene, enquired of us if anything was wrong. 'Wrong!' howled O'Liver stamping. 'I have been asleep. Which as you may know is kinsman to death, trance and madness. That is what is wrong!'

Came Friday, seated among a clutch of fellow auditioners, some hypnotised by the wall opposite, a couple muttering, others scrutinising the floor, none wanting a drag from the illicit fag I had lit up, my mind, feelings and body were at one: excited, yes, but untroubled.

We had chosen for my ensemble, I and the secretary, a Prince of Wales check, three-piece suit. A dark red rose, bought at Covent Garden, in my buttonhole, a pastel yellow and green tie, from Oxford Street, neatly knotted round my neck, my suede boots, Army Surplus Store, scrubbed tidy with a bath brush, both speeches confidently waiting to be given trippingly on my tongue, I loitered there, puffing my cigarette, keen to get on with it.

'Mr Peter O'Toole.' It was my turn.

'Good morning,' I called to the silent row of shadows and faces seated behind the length of a long table at the far end of a large room. From two lamps standing at either side of the table strong light focused on the area where we were to do our pieces. A murmur of answering good mornings came to me as I took my place, announced what I intended to speak, took a deep breath and then blurted out my two speeches as feelingly and clearly as I could.

That is all I can recall. That and walking towards the door saying, 'Good morning,' again.

Among the return good mornings a voice asked me how tall I was, another shadow wanted to know if I had had any professional experience, the face on top of the substantial figure of Sir Kenneth scowled at me and invited me to take a seat downstairs in the hall. 'Six foot two. No. Thank you, sir.'

Sergeant was in his guardroom at the door, Bernard Shaw was looking well at the foot of the stairway, I popped out for a breath of fresh air and a smoke. Beneath the grin of Thalia and the glum Melpomene my pacing and puffing encountered the to-ing and fro-ing of a young man, dark-haired, dark-suited, two or three years older than me, with a confident, worldly manner who, as we chimed together in chat, turned out also to have been asked to wait. Bob, call him, polite, correct, quick on the draw with the silver cigarette case and the lighter, if at all anxious it was well concealed and after a while, we agreed that, win, lose or draw, we would have a lunchtime drink together.

Shortly, Sergeant popped out and summoned Bob inside, leaving me alone to plod up and down, up and down, smoking, pondering, attempting to be debonair.

Sergeant again.

Me.

Into an office where a pretty secretary lady tells me that my audition went very well, would I please turn up again in two weeks' time, here's another batch of audition pieces, one of which I must mug up, should I be contemplating official assistance with my fees or a scholarship even, here are various forms to fill in, a booklet to read, and was there anything else that she could do?

Only give me a kiss and point me in the direction of the nearest telephone, you trim and efficient little dumpling, here's a rose to remember me by, the next two weeks might prove quite lively, so could I please have your office telephone number, the better to remain in touch, thank you, do, please, give Sir Kenneth my regards and tell him that his blood is worth bottling.

Standing by Bernard Shaw, Bob was waiting for me. We bade Sergeant *au revoir* and strolled to the nearest pub.

A fount of useful information, Bob turned out to be, on methods and subtleties involved in claiming government assistance for higher education; more, he drove a car. Rare, that, in an England still rationed and restricted seven years after the war, with dogs in office yapping at us that austerity was a moral imperative. Bollocks.

———————

TELL US: sorry, babies; we have won the bloody war, the nation has gone broke doing that, over fifty million men, women and children have been killed, most of them civilians, six in every hundred of us here in England have had our homes bombed to buggery, money's scarce, food's scarce, petrol's scarce, there are very few restaurants and cheese has just been rationed again. Ideologues are in government, both Stalin and Django Reinhardt the jazz man are dead, in the discernible future we do not see the return of the flying bombs and the rockets which from 1944 to 1945 so brutally tormented those in the south of England, nor of the high explosive and incendiary bombs which between 1940 and 1941 nearly destroyed us all.

We can offer you quite a lot of hard work for modest rewards, you must most certainly scratch up what fun you can. Big bands are blowing out sweet swinging dance music. Boffins are producing an improved gadget which encourages women to take on themselves the onus of contraception, so for the blokes it can be farewell to the French letter and whatever radical effects this may have on society as we know it the poking should be mighty.

It will take a while for the multitude of functionaries whom expedience considered wise to appoint in roles of authority, while maintaining vital rigours and discipline during the crisis of wartime England, to relax their appointed grip. You see, those in whom there has been temporarily engendered the authority down, responsibility up, master, servant, officer, trooper, governor, groveller, dogs obeyed in office spirit will only with aching reluctance realise that they were born to be no one in particular, because this authority, it's heady stuff. Hitler knew that; above all he knew that. He made everyone at least an auxiliary policeman with powers of seize and search and the entire nation marched around giving or receiving orders or obedience. So, do you see, that for many it will probably take a while to realise that their days of domination, subjugation and power are over; gone those days when a mere, 'Put that light out,' uttered from under a tin hat would extinguish flame. Be patient, in some it may never go away. It may breed. The cunning will of necessity desire it. The better way is gently to disarm it, go round it, flatter it, saying bollocks is scarcely enough and do not, please, hit it on the head with a coke-hammer. You will find that digs, cigarettes, beer and whiskey, are at present available and though far from cheap are, as luxuries go, comparatively inexpensive. More. We intend to put the arm on Argentina to squeeze out of her a few tins of bully beef for the Sunday roast. Fuck the begrudgers; don't let the bastards grind you down, and what price England against Australia for the Ashes?

———————

Not only did Bob thus particularly own a car but also he would be aiming in the direction I most needed to get to sharpish. Indeed, after having had Bob mark my card on matters high educational, it was urgently clear that I had a lot of letters to write, people to see, things to do, eggs to lay, and that I had better be off and doing.

Arrangements with the appropriate powers had been made. At the oral examination, with three senior educators as my interlocutors, questions were asked of me about the plays of T. S. Eliot and my views on Shakespeare's *Twelfth Night*. Having read, loved and tussled much with Eliot's poetry but having neither read nor seen one of his blessed plays, that took some fancy footwork but we remained vertical and, as I could, would and may punch my weight on behalf of *Twelfth Night*, their earholes took a pounding on that much loved subject, costumes, scenery, music and all, and, in my view, at the death, I had won on points.

And yet. One didn't know and, what is more, even if stone lucky, one would still not know that for weeks. Yes. Then there was the second audition. Still, if the conditions had not radically changed, the choice of material was apt and the ability to put it down on the day had remained sound, well then, chance might be.

Brightside: a fair roll of the blue and green folding lettuce safely trousered, enough to bed and feed you, keep you supple, warm, stimulated and to pay fees in advance for a term at the RADA. Therefore, it is down to the second audition. Right. What the fuck is this?

It is squat, nasty, khaki, small; it is a little, brutal, official envelope. It bears my name and its contents tell me that my being a reservist in the Royal Navy means that shortly I needs must present my lovely young body to a dockyard at Portsmouth where it will be wrapped in wool and tarpaulin, shoved into bell-bottoms and will then be heaved onto the iron quarter deck of one of Her Majesty's warships.

Now; it was the time of the Korean War. They were using real bullets out there.

IT IS altogether possible that Hunsbeck and environs, the area in which I had lived during most of the war, was among the least-bombed industrial areas in Europe. We were bombed only three times. Seventy-seven people were killed. Collectively, the atrocity as news value could not have earned more than a line in the national newspapers. The destruction by bombing and burning of London and its citizens, the devastation in so many of the cities and towns of England, Scotland, Wales and Ireland, did, in that time, eventually earn no more than a paragraph in a newspaper, a few words on the wireless, a black and white film clip on a newsreel.

My arrival back at Hunsbeck in 1940 had been cheered up by a bombing raid. It had been grotesquely alarming. The second time, well. Did you ever see the ball coming right from the bat, right up into the air, coming to you and sure to land there or thereabouts where you are now and you must catch it? Well, it's the same when you sense that the bomb is going to drop on your head, only we couldn't see it, but we could hear it.

We were crouched, my mother, my sister, my father and I, in a cellar during an air raid. The giant scream from the bomb as it came down became so loud that it was insupportable. We were in terror. My mother winced so deeply before she threw herself over my sister that her face then will stay with me for ever: next, my dotty old Pop came flying over me, I could smell his tobacco and his linen but, mercy, the catch was not on, the bomb did not land on us but on a library and natural history museum two miles away.

The following morning I stood on a lip of the crater made by the bomb, inhaled dust and the bitter reek of fires and detonated explosives, looked at the ruin and wreckage of the tumbled building, the wild scattering of burned books, the crazy sprawl of a busted, broken, stuffed giraffe unremarked by the firemen digging and stumbling through a shambles of shattered brick and stone.

The next visit, well, my little sister was not with us, the poor scrap had gone to a hospital. After the night when we had been sure that we were going to cop it the child had been stifled by a dreadful choke of asthma, had lost all her black curly hair, had been taken away by ambulance, had been given a trachcotomy and when we went to see her, the girl was canopied by glass and breathing through a rubber tube stuck into her throat.

Came the next visit. Mummy stayed in the cellar dispensing tea, cigarettes, counsel and comfort to dismayed, frightened neighbours while the old man and I crept out unnoticed. Perhaps the ball player in Father insisted that, however improbable, he must have a look at what was being thrown at him. Perhaps we both wanted to see the great bright searchlights flaying the night sky, see the anti-aircraft shells burst, the startling shooting of tracer bullets, hear the alarms, the crump of explosions, the high aching drones from above.

He had opened the door, right enough; the door was open and we both stood at the dark doorway peering up at the sky when, suddenly, for a long instant everything went astonishingly white, white white white; this whiteness ended abruptly as it began, replaced by an almighty bang, followed immediately by a silent, immense warm force which lifted the pair of us up and floated us half-way up the flight of stairs running up behind us.

There we had sat, unharmed, alarmed, shocked but not speechless. Daddy began a protracted conversation with Jesus and his blessed Mother. My mother entered the scene, shut the door, made all secure, scolded us, kissed us, and, after a clucking while, the three of us sat there, our arms round each other, perhaps weeping, perhaps praying, perhaps silent, alive, though, alive, alive o o, and certainly getting used to it.

Nor did I see many deaths during the war. A couple of stiffs and one man killed before my eyes. Saw many of the wounded, the maimed and the blind, though. Stood forlorn with mothers and fathers whose children had been killed or had gone missing. Had read the papers, seen the newsreels, heard the wireless as we set to the killing of fifty million people in the world war of '39 to '45 at a rate of well over a hundred thousand each week for six years.

IT HAD therefore been no hardship to join His Majesty's Navy in that time of peace when I was eighteen. It had been a rigorous, tough, instructive and deeply funny time those two years that I had spent bouncing about on the dip.

Alas, His Majesty had not survived my time in his navy. The unknowable burden of being a good king during the most bitterly critical time that his country had known in a thousand years had broken his health and one night, a night when I was sailing far away on the Baltic Sea, His slender Majesty had handed in his dinner pail and had gone to reside with the morning stars.

That was then though, Toad, that was then; this is now. I am on the verge of doing an amazing leap onto the stage. What means the daughter of this dead good king that I must now rejoin what is now Her Royal Navy? Surely there are others better fitted for these hornpipes and manoeuvres? Why rope in a poofy old mummer to litter quite the wheelhouse, the spinnaker and the bo'sun's chair? Then, my gracious lady, there is this fucking Korea lark. Did not one of your late father's frigates, only a short while since, go skidding up and down the river Yangtse, popping off guns right into the Chinese mainland? Have you anything of the like in mind for me? Once, ma'am, when I was eight, during an incendiary raid, the bombs made no bang, their fireloads often failed to ignite, such occurrences counted for little, I stood screaming for a gun or a dagger or a rock to attack back at these monstrous barbarians who were hoping to annihilate us. But that was then. I am now nearly twenty-one, less frantic, my sights are set on comparatively peaceful purposes, could you not, pray, just send an atom bomb and leave me be to get on with this tricky business of becoming an actor? No? Ah well.

Still I stood, that dreadful buff envelope opened in my hand, knowing that I must down to the sea again, but when? Not for a couple of months. Time enough to plot and plan and do. A little G.K. Chesterton, a touch of Henry James was what we had chosen to give the RADA examiners, they had been practically the only words that we had spoken for a week, a dark suit of one's own we had thought to be fitting for round two, a maroon-coloured tie, a beautiful cream shirt bearing thin red stripes, with only one previous occupant, my father, highly polished black shoes, one's own property, and we bought the rose for my buttonhole on the day of the race.

After discharging my pieces, in the same large room, to what appeared to be the same large tableful of judges, I was treading wonderingly down the RADA stairs, heading for Bernard Shaw, when a tall man with a beautiful deep voice strode out of the audition room and caught up with me on a landing.

'Look here, look here, look here,' he had said. 'We think quite highly of you in there, quite highly, quite highly, quite highly. You have auditioned for us very well. Very well, very well, very well. Tell me. Do I hear a slight lisp? A slight lisp, a slight lisp, a slight lisp?'

Indeed you do hear a slight lisp, tall stranger with a fine handsome head who repeats much of what you say resonantly, articulately and twenty-nine times, you do indeed hear a slight lisp. The mercy is that I have still a whole tongue with which to lisp at all. Did I not, less than one year ago, almost leave half of it on a rugby field? If you have played or seen or heard of the game then you will know that if the team opposing you is composed of police constables who cannot play the game for toffee but who are big bastards, strong, fast, fit, hard and nasty all over; that if your team can field only sailors, not fit, not fast, easy-going and only nasty when goaded; that if the scrimmages are slaughterhouses, the line-outs only opportunities for bare-knuckled battery, and your skipper has some nous, that he may elect to avoid these forward-play set-pieces by calling for a sprinkling of Garryowens. The up and under. By booting the ball far and high you have time to run, get under it, and if you cleanly gather the pill, or touch it even, it means that you and the rest of your fifteen, even fifteen puffed and coughing rolling sailors, are onside, toddling in the direction of the enemy's line, that the coppers needs must run back into their own half, most of them will not be facing you, their fullback, as are most, is not supremely happy under the highball; that superior skills at ruck and maul, the loose ball, the leap and tap back, the swift pass, the dummy, the jink, the half gap and the dip and dive in at the flag might turn the trick nicely for your seagoing side.

The skipper suggested that we not kick for touch but spray

up leather at the bastards. This we did. The luck of the bounce bounded our way, there was much skilful, stylish thieving, ripping and smuggling, accurate passing of the ball along the line, our fullback made the extra man and by half time, having run in three tries, we had points on the board. Three tries. Not one had been converted because not one of our team was any good at kicking goals but we did have one man who tried, missed all three, and was adjudged by us, his fellows, as we sucked our oranges soaked in brandy at half-time, to be a big girl's blouse who might yet cost us the game.

In the second half it had all turned out to be horribly different.

Big Lily Law had sussed our play; sussed it, noted it, had decided they would flatter us by imitation and, proceeding rapidly in our direction, compelled us to assist them in their enquiries as to whether or not we could live through the next forty of the dirtiest minutes that they could muster. Their rugby had been no better. No better, no better, no better. Neither was their team's foul temper. Foul temper, foul temper, foul temper.

Badly aggrieved at being three scores down, miffed was Hedda Handcuffs, not pleased, eager to try this here up and under caper on these lolling sailor boys, so puny or young or tubby or old or suchlike, who had, with their skill, made Hedda seem clumsy and who deserved no more than to be ground down, right down, down into the ground, ground right down into the background. Up and under! Oh, Lord, love you.

When the leather is hoisted high into the air, kicked there by a huge policeman's big foot, one who is fond, and will in time grow fonder, of kicking balls hard, the ball goes up and stays up for quite a while. Now, he among the sailors who must catch the lofted knacker is usually the fifteen spot, the fullback. Not only must his eye be stuck on that ball, he must also rapidly assess at what spot the ball will descend to earth, get to that spot, catch the ball spinning right down at him and hope to have it safely in his arms before the kicker and the opposition arrive to bury him. When the catcher and the kicker and the opposition arrive at the ball at the same time, the number fifteen, the fullback, the ocean-going seaman now gone for the ball, usually takes quite a lot of slipper.

Our man certainly did and then there were fourteen.

Before substitutes were invented, fourteen thirsty matelots faced fifteen rampant bogeys with thirty minutes to go.

The kidney punch, the eye gouge, the heel-of-the-hand jab under the nose, the knee in the crutch, the ear bite, the foot stamp, the head butt in the face are some of the refinements of the game seldom practised in training. We had never practised them, but, then, we had never trained. It was known that our goal kicker drank horse liniment before a match so as to smell fit but that was about the size of it. The policemen, though, were adept at these unorthodox subtleties and had obviously cultivated them assiduously.

Our response when it came, as come it did, lacked that polish which training can make gleam in a side, but compensated for this lack by its freshness and spontaneity of expression as a pack of wounded mariners burst onto their persecutors to smash, bash, thump, wallop, squeeze, tear, behead, dismember and break. For a while the ball was superfluous, whistles were blown, flags waved, chaps in duffel coats pulled players off other players, even players pulled players off players, blokes with buckets and sponges attended, nursie, lovely sight, jiggled onto the field, probably bearing smelling salts, accompanying the ambulancemen with the stretcher.

Fourteen baying coppers versus thirteen very cross mariners and twenty minutes to go.

The ideal referee is unbiased, schooled in the rules, sharp-eyed and fleet; by awarding the opposition two penalties in front of the posts for our alleged foul play, the official in charge of this minor game of rugby union football showed us that he owned none of these virtues. What's more, their team had a nasty who could and did kick goals. This not only closed up the score quite a bit but also would have been a lesson to our toerag, who couldn't kick pussy, had he not been asleep under a blanket at the side of the pitch.

An old pink gin in gold braid garumphed, 'Tigerish, Navy!' my wingman took up the indisposed fullback's position; this left me still far from the heaving, grunting, bloodstained scrimmagers but with the curious onus of being an out centre to half of what had formerly been a four-man three-quarter line. Not that rigid positioning was the rule, it was Rafferty's rule at the moment as the ball became yet again superfluous and the field was adorned with ructions.

'O'Toole. Go to full back.' This is unreasonable. Fullbacks are born entirely as fullbacks and can be fullbacks only. They must have an immense capacity to withstand and to dispense the most brutal physical contact. To run and catch cleanly the steepling, punted, heavy, greasy leather as Old Bill arrives in a rampant platoon to crush you under his pounding fists and feet. To avoid nimbly these butchers, to balance, to assess instantly the options, to run and jink and link, to break and pass, to drill expertly the ball forty yards from the foot and safely into touch.

One is only born to these skills and iron courage, it is folly, surely, for any captain to think that his mere appointment of this centre three-quarter to a fullback's position might immediately invest him with these uniquely cherished qualities.

Captain, my captain, I can tackle when I must and be tackled when I am, but my infinite preference is to stay away from all these mighty men who maul and ruck and scrum; to be astonishingly alive when these splendid warriors produce the ball at the rear of their fearsome, scrummed deliberations, to be already travelling as the scrum half flings the long pass to the nimble fly half, who will draw his man and feed his in centre, who will commit his counterpart before flicking it to me, who will motor, who will go round or inside or through his marker, will draw the full back and will then time a swift accurate pass to the guts of his wingman who will then fly in at the flag. That sort of thing.

There is no wingman. I am the full back. There are yet twelve sailors facing fourteen policemen, none of whom will give an inch let alone a quarter, and there are ten of those long minutes to go.

Here comes the pill, get under the fucking thing; got it; trample of approaching boots; steady; now hoof the fucker as high and as far as you have ever hoofed a fucker, there she goes. Piss off!

They have not scored again, nor have we, keep the bastards out seems to be the tactic. Here comes the old pill again. Whoops, Jug, I love thee! Stowed safely under the arm and we just avoid a crushing from a cauliflowered Lily, steam away from a squad of berserkers, nip inside for a step or two and then hoof her up, up, up and under her we go!

No score but we shoved the bastards back under their own posts, that's ground gained, that's time used well and off we go again.

It must be full-time, that bent referee should blow the whistle, but here comes a horde of beastly bogies with the knacker at their feet, 'Die with it, Navy,' howls Pink Gin from in touch.

You look at nothing but the ball and, when it's a yard or so from you, you fall on it, you wrap your loving arms around it and you never let it go.

A bootful of policeman found my head a better thing to kick than the ball, and when I woke up my jaw was in bits, my back teeth down my throat and my tongue bitten and split in half. This frolic occurred seconds before the final whistle blew, signifying that whatever game it was that we had been playing was over, and that we had by no means lost it.

Tongues cannot be stitched they must be clamped. This meant, after the gyp had died down, quiet relaxation and recuperation away from this hardy shipboard life, hilarious disfigurement of my speech, 'Ee ay I ah um or', please may I have some more, a comfy billet and, yes, nursie to feel my pulse.

The upshot is that I was left with a considerably thicker tongue. Thicker tongue, thicker tongue, thicker tongue. Which is already wagging and tripping and licking better and better each day.

'That's very good,' said the tall smiling man who immediately after my second audition at the RADA had caught up with me on a landing of the stairs there. 'Very good, very good, very good,' and then he was gone.

'PROPAGANDA! Propaganda! Propaganda!' Prison had agreed with him, thick set he stands, his raincoat belted over his plus twos, his trilby in his hand, his body and features forcefully composed; the face stern, the attitude hard; the gormlessness is gone, the splenetic crank is gone; gone, too, the undernourished thinness, the pointed moustache, the wisp of beard, the gaunt, neurotic, silly face, the servility, the fawning, the cringing eagerness to comply with the imperatives of High Command; this strong, determined man standing here outside Landsberg prison on the day of his release from it, is a leader, is a desperado, is an author, a painter, an architect, a revolutionary, an insurrectionist, one who has, and will again, dare all; he is enormously intelligent and brave, he is what you have been looking for, my own folk: he is your Führer.

See it for yourself, the snap taken in late December 1924 of Hitler when he was thirty-five, you may find it amusing.

The left arm is healed. When the bullets flew outside the Feldherrnhalle during the Beerhall Putsch of '23, Scheubner-Richter, mentor and tutor to Hitler, went down early and went down dead as stone. A White Russian, German patriot from the Baltic States, Shovehalfpenny-Rictus, a spy, an engineer, a diplomat, an actor, a busted toff, a confidence trickster, this polymath had in solidarity linked arms with Hitler and when he hit the dogshelf hard he took Hitler with him. His death spasm caused him to yank Alf's left arm out of its socket and as they both fell the arm was further damaged by being broken above the elbow as he heavily fell on it. My guess is that Hitler thought he had been shot.

The wrench from the shoulder must have been exciting, the

gunfire an old familiar, a shot deadman hanging onto him where once had trod Shovehalfpenny, may probably have been novel to him but the all-fall-down game was nothing new. The putschists had been in wide marching formation so many were blown down; sixteen killed, many wounded, some seriously, Fat Hermann among them. When the firing stopped, the remainder three thousand stampeded out of there. Meldeganger Hitler, finely tuned to the gallop after surviving four years of bullets in the trenches at the front, showed them the way, Fat Hermann, wounds and all, turned a nifty ankle and they both got to their getaway cars and got away promptly. Goering scarpered over the bumps, eventually fetching up in Italy, Shatterhand Hitler fled to Putzi's pad thirty miles away, was attended by a doctor, spoke of ruin and suicide, plonked his aching head on Frau Helene's satin lap, let loose the waterworks and waited to be arrested.

Call him Shatterhand in homage to a favourite author of Alf's: Karl May. Shatterhand is the brooding, brainy, fearless paleface whose singular adventures are the stuff of many of the American Cowboy and Indian novels written by the German Karl May.

Prison is behind us now in 1925. We have learned much in it. The passages of Schopenhauer and Nietzsche that we had discovered to be pertinent to our person, philosophy and propaganda have been learned by heart, our phenomenal memory will in the future allow us to quote these authors by the pageful when we consider the occasion for their recital to be apt. Regular, solid grub has helped us to put on weight. This suits us. We look fitter, stronger, handsome even, we have more bottom and more stomach for the coming and continuing struggle.

Alas, we have had to learn anew that which was already known to us: successful criminals don't get caught. From now on all that we do in the pursuit of power will appear to be done as though the law allows it. Nazi supporters who are caught breaking the law will be disowned. Nazi supporters who do not unconditionally worship their Führer will be murdered. We are no longer the prophet of the

Nazi godhead, we are the Nazi godhead itself. The book that we have written while in prison, *Mein Kampf*, presents a version of ourself, from childhood to the present, that exactly corresponds with the way in which we will rigorously conduct ourself from this moment of our setting out from jail to the instant of our death.

If you read the newspapers, listen to the talk in the cafés and the beerhalls, are privy to the hot gossip going around the police, the army, the judiciary, the civil service, the political groupings, then you will know the word is that Adolf Hitler at his trial was found guilty of being a great German patriot. One whose intellectual genius, tongue of angels, quick trigger finger, and unsparing animal energy had been entirely at the service of the Fatherland. Who had flung himself at the hordes of Bolshevists and Jews threatening to crush and poison the superior spirit of the German and by his wildly noble example had shown the authorities and the citizens of Germany the true nature of their souls; if they only would aspire to it.

Yes, the guards, the governor, the police, had shown great sympathy towards us and our cause, but we want much more than their sympathy, we want, and will patiently get, first their adherence to us and then their absolute obedience.

Most important. We have a lawful and ideal organ to grind. We are the owner and publisher of our own newspaper, the *Volkischer Beobachter*, *My Own Folks' Gazette*, with it we will spread our vividly conceived propaganda. Propaganda, propaganda, propaganda.

Hank the Snapper has the very good idea of transforming it into a picture newspaper. That is good. Bold type, dramatic photographs, plangent articles. We have six themes to pound into eyes and heads. Ourself. The leadership principle. Jew hatred. German racial superiority. Expansion to the East. The iniquitous treaty of Versailles.

First, though, the leadership principle; the rest will then follow as surely as obedience follows command. Start with our body and its guard. We shall appoint Wrecker Schreck to be its governor.

This guard will be composed of seven thugs in an ascending scale of seniority with Schreck at the top. Responsibility and obedience will flow up, authority and command will spread down. There will, of course, be a deputy leader, as there will, of course, be seven deputy guards. Among whom, too, responsibility goes up, authority presses down. On our instructions the Nazi party will provide a department to deal with all affairs relating to the Führer's bodyguard; Esser the Messer will command this department. We shall draw up a secret protocol which appoints Weber the Shark as supervisor extraordinary to our body and its guards. It will, of course, be necessary to maintain an objective vigilance over this entire structure. For this sensitive and secretive post there really is no better man than Clocker Maurice.

Among this superbly disciplined élite, promotion or demotion will naturally depend upon merit or its lack. Anyone who suspects another of giving less than total effort to the vital task of guarding our body must immediately employ the means that we shall provide for contacting ourself, the supreme authority, privately: and we shall then assess such information and assert ourself ruthlessly.

So you see, my own folk, those of you who are led will own security, moral ease, the theoretical possibility of you yourself becoming a leader and sharing a portion of this authority without responsibility. Your chief risk will be in your struggle for the favour of a higher authority, but you surely may reduce this risk to a minimum by demonstrating absolute obedience towards this higher authority.

Simple. The leadership principle.

As we ourself, the absolute supreme leader, take the whole responsibility for everything on ourself alone, we assume an awesome burden, for no one but ourself can call us to account.

It is our unalterable intention to bind every strand of the Nazi organisation into this gripping leadership principle and then what a mighty struggle for obedience there will be.

'SILENT NIGHT, holy night'. Perhaps they all sang that song that Christmas Eve at Putzi's pad in 1924 when Alf, sprung from the nick, returned to the house where he had been arrested, over a year before, to spend the holy holiday there. It's possible. After all, up to the age of seventeen Alf had taken singing and piano lessons, was fond of crooning out the odd burst of a ditty and, indeed, the family Hitler were known in Linz as being friends of song. Whatever, he certainly thrilled the four year old son of the house with his brilliant mimicry of artillery fire, that and his famous set piece for children: Alf's impersonation of a railway train starting up and chuffing out of a station with its whistle blowing.

Later, when no one was looking, he had again rubbed his moustache along Frau Helene's lap, moaning that he wanted someone like her to look after him and had been reproved by her for being a naughty boy.

No. Being thought of as a naughty boy would not do. He was a man who at that time understood the mechanics of this interesting experiment in government, democracy, better than any other man alive. No man could better abuse the hypocrisies and corruption inherent in the system. Political genius he was, one who could divine and exploit all weaknesses, all strengths, all prejudice, all beliefs, all frustrations, gullibilities, passions, all that was conservative or liberal or radical or hateful, one for whom large sections of the voting mob would serve as spectators, as audience, as congregation, as worshippers. A world historical figure; destined to lead his nation out of their distress, their defeat, their humiliation, their destitution; their military, political, social and spiritual disillusionment and to make them yet again a barbarously mighty people.

Will his bottle stand the test, though, will the pucker hold?

His private manner has more confidence than we are used to: until recently the only consistent element in his public and personal behaviour was that disturbingly insane excitement over matters great and small, now he is less strident, chatty even, given to charming smiles.

His costume has changed radically again.

The buzz from the squeezer has it that Alf was seen swanning about the exercise yard, giving out with the gestures and the chunter, wearing a pair of those short leather trousers with cross straps over the shoulders of the blouse, and stockings to the knee.

One wonders if he wore that little pork pie trilby with a shaving brush stuck in the band.

He has been enormously popular in that fortress prison at Landsberg. One who had been wounded but had escaped the slaughter of the comrades outside the Feldherrnhalle, had been persuaded to give up his hunger strike by dozens of colleagues who had pleaded that without him the movement would be leaderless, who had then begun to eat with relish, receiving so many hampers of food that after La Belle Helene had called on him she had described his cell as looking like a delicatessen. Who had realised more swiftly than others that the bloody fiasco of the beerhall *putsch* was being generally received as a magnificently heroic act of daredevilry giving martyrdom, nobility and glory to the Nazis. Whose strange sister Angela had said of him after a visit that his spirit and soul were again at a high level. That his poor arm, though getting better, was still giving him gyp. That the loyalty of all towards him was deeply moving. That what he had accomplished was solid as rock and that the goal and the victory were only a question of time. That the quality called on him; that while she was there a count had dropped in with a parcel from the family Wagner.

His accusers had loaded all the responsibility and the blame for the insurrection on him. He had realised this to be a big blessing and had bravely accepted his role as mastermind and firebrand of the *putsch*.

At his trial had he not with power, wit and dignity impressed all? In his final address to the judges had he not said that though they may pronounce him guilty of high treason a thousand times, the goddess of the eternal court of history will smile and tear to tatters this verdict, for she will acquit him?

When he had been weighed off for five years had not all the lags and screws cheered him as a hero when he re-entered his flowery dell, cell? Isn't the word out that the coppers and the mouthpieces and the beaks who had sympathised with him before the rumpus, had been so impressed with the way in which he had kept his mouth shut on certain essential concerns touching them somewhat sensitively, that an arrangement had been made which assured him that at most he would serve only two years, certainly not five, and hadn't he been sprung after only nine months?

What was the first thing that he did when he began his bird, birdlime, time? Began writing a book. Called it 'My four and a half years of struggle against lies, stupidity and cowardice'. Clocker Maurice tried his hand at tapping the typewriter for him but those long fingers fitted better round the neck of whoever it was that he was strangling than they did clicking the keys and so Fräulein Anna Hess took over. Very efficient she had proved, too, and she persuaded him to abbreviate the title. It is now called just 'My Struggle', *Mein Kampf*.

Not that he had ignored the social obligations that his being in the nick placed on him. As many visitors as he wished for six to eight hours a throw, the joint was thronged with soldiers, politicians in toppers, writers, all sorts of important sods from all over the shop. And women. Lordy. The odour of crumpet and cologne was driving the time-serving lags crackers. Someone said that the birds had looked at him in a devotional ecstasy, whatever that means, they had certainly looked as though they were foaming at the crutch. He had just bowed and kissed their hands and listened to their prattle. Not Clocker, though. Clocker had laid some of that devotional ecstasy lark on the head screw's curly headed daughter and her squeaks had been heard by the lags pruning turnips in the kitchen garden. Alf had just laughed when he heard. He's no prude, you know, he encourages the lads to give the whiskey and the women a tanking. He's fond of a small jug himself. Smokes a little snout, too. Not too keen on woofters, mind, but if someone grasses on them to him he just cocks a deaf 'un. Clocker found a duplicating machine lying loose about the place and so Alf was able to wank out a prison newspaper. He called it the *Landsberg Honorary Citizen* and wrote all the leading articles as well as doing the drorings at which he's a dab hand.

When the news that ten Nazis had been elected to Parliament floated into the nick, all Alf had said was that from now on all Nazis would just have to hold their noses and enter Parliament against the others' deputies, Marxist and all, that from now on there would be a new policy, that there would be no more attempts at armed coups and that if outvoting them took longer than outshooting them, well, the results would be guaranteed by their own constitution! He's a boy. There had been a bit of a shock when he resigned as Nazi boss but Fräulein Anna said that Alf would appoint a dud in his place and then just watch as his rivals formed sewing bees all over Germany, began to bicker and squabble, stick needles into each other's eyes and then wait for them all to splinter into bits. After his release he would choose the pieces that best suited him, glue them together into a desirable shape and then become governor again. You and me would call it doing sweet fuck all but he calls it organic growth.

There had been a nasty moment when it looked as though he might be deported back to Austria but someone in the Ministry of Justice must have been straightened and the block was put on that. Wrecker had it from Clocker that Messer had wheeled in a mouthpiece who had advised Alf to lose his Austrian nationality and become stateless. Don't know quite what that means but I suppose that if you don't come from anywhere and the authorities want to send you somewhere they might find there's nowhere that will take you. When his parole came everybody, bar Alf, had wept, even the governor. Odd sight that must have been, toerags, villains and murderers dabbing at their hooters with itsy-bitsy hankies. That spell in the squeezer had done him nothing but good, I reckon. He strutted out of it shining with glory.

Patricia O'Toole. My sister.
London 1961.

———

When he was six years of age the days had been glorious for little Bright eyed Alf. Daddy Hitler had set up clink below the ranges of mountains at Lambach, by the river Traun, a trim little town owning a Benedictine monastery, set in a Wagnerian wilderness of peak and pine and regularly visited by the chuff-chuff steaming from Munich in Germany, rattling through the gaps in Austria and rolling on to Linz.

Being the quick, friendly and able little son of the chief customs officer may have had its charms. When I was a boy my mate Jumbo had had an uncle who was a detective inspector. Jumbo had been accorded a wary respect, more so because he had been a whiz at snooker, could handle himself tastily and was an evil big sod.

Organised sport of any sort had been ignored by the educators at Lambach but numeracy and literacy were held high. Little Alf had excelled at all his school subjects, revelled with his mates in their rough outdoor play and his Mum and old Dad had doted on the little bugger. His father's daughter Angela, Alf's sister by another mother, seems always to have worshipped him in a fascinated way.

After a splendid year in the one classroom of a school for infants, Alf became a pupil at the Benedictine Monastery School and from his entering to his leaving it in his tenth year, he had been popular with both teachers and boys, excelled at all subjects and had led his peers in games of goodies and baddies through the Nibelung Forest. He sang in the choir but did not acquire too much devotional soapiness, his joyful chatter was remarked as was his ability to listen, absorb and retain what had been said, and even the remote and inbred, suspicious mountainy men and women were amused by his mischievous bossiness.

When Daddy, taking Alf and the family with him, upped the beehive and buzzed off to Linz and to retirement, the idyll had ended. In a rural suburb near the railway of the great parallelogram, Linz, for a while all went fairly well for Alf. He took his hurdles all right: the move, the death of his six year old brother Edmund, the new surroundings, the new neighbours, school, companions. Although not top pupil as he had been at Lambach, he continued to excel at school. A snap taken at the time shows him in his cock of the walk pose, fair lording it over his classmates but, as puberty and the age of eleven arrived, he was sent to a posh secondary high school in central Linz.

Things were never the same again.

The sons of the doctors, professors, lawyers and like professionals who attended the Realschule at Linz, had not been overly impressed by this bumpkin, Hitler, A., child of some obscure retired customs man from up an alp, nor, it seems, were his teachers. Competition was stiff, standards high and no one appears to have been able sympathetically to tap Alf's undoubted abilities.

Indolent, erratic, unreliable, loud-mouthed and coarse, with the leaping exception of gymnastics, he had been at no time able fully to apprehend a discipline, though for four more long, humiliating years he continued attending school.

When Alf was fourteen his father fell off the perch, six months later darling Angela married, one Raubal, a customs man whom Alf loathed, and at fifteen he transferred to a country boarding school at Steyr, where he staged a brief, feeble rally, improving slightly his sums and his geography.

At sixteen, having persuaded his mother of his need for a private education, he had quit school for good. Thus liberated from painful classrooms, Alf could be seen bowling along the boulevards of Linz wearing a cutaway coat, spats, a high collar, a flowing cravat and high-stepping it as he twiddled his walking cane with the ivory tip.

For the next eleven years, Adolf Hitler, at Linz, at Vienna, at Munich, exists to us only as a scarce-remembered crank. He had money enough to live on and some to spend. At times he increased the kitty by applying himself to a canvas. He painted pictures to adorn frames. Yes. A framemaker needed paintings which would attract the eye to the frame. Hitler was his man.

That is a rare talent, that is a sublime mediocrity, to paint on canvas a scene which in no way detracts from the tone and symmetry of the frame.

Of course this gifted young man came to the attention of other framemakers and, when he chose, Alf could so particularly dab dab away to earn himself a few extra bucks.

The only shaky year that he suffered had been when he was twenty. On the trot avoiding military service, he had had to keep his head down while dodging the Austrian police. His pal Gustle had gone back to Linz, joined the army and, after a year's service had returned to Vienna to find that Alf had bolted.

History sleuths have traced Hitler's movements, fetching up a dozen and more addresses of doss-houses where he had some nights stayed. It is possible that during summer he had occasionally kipped on park benches. Christmas found him in the queue for soup at an asylum for the shelterless but after this he moved into a men's hostel on the Meldemannstrasse. The hostel cost more than would a rented room but had provided a cosy billet, a kitchen, a cafeteria and the sanctuary of a reading room. There, among the bogus barons, cashiered majors, hawkers, pedlars, drifters and con men who regarded the hostel as the Ritz of its like, for the next three years and more, Adolf Hitler had sat on his seat at the table by the window, occasionally painting, incessantly talk, talk, talking, and talking yet again.

The good news was that Raubal, the despised customs and tax man who had married the strange Angela, had died. Alf and Angela came to a sensible arrangement about money: Alf switched the fraudulently acquired orphan's pension to Angela, in return he was to cop the bulk of Hunchback Joanna Hitler's or Hiedler's or Hüttler's estate when she snuffed it, which she very shortly did.

This happy circumstance left Alf adequately provided with money until he reached the age of twenty-five.

Fugitive, timid, he flitted about, consistent traits being a maniacal sensitivity and a deep need to present a respectable, educated, bourgeois front, an attitude which often came unstuck. Hanisch, Alf's dodgy mate who had hawked the paintings for him, years later put down on paper his thoughts about his curious, provincial, former crony, Alf, and in 1938 Alf had him murdered.

In all those years, from the age of eleven to the age of twenty-eight, it seems that in society the future Führer had been something less than a goer.

ONLY IN 1917, in glorious, bloody Flanders, do we hear of Hitler being suffered gladly again. The officers and men of his regiment regard him with affection and respect, for he has proved himself to be a brave and good soldier.

Odd cove, mind, writes poetry, attempts a refined manner, has a pet dog, a quaint line in amusingly provocative chatter, the chaps say it's a relief when the firing starts for it shuts up Hitler, however, it is 1918 and for untiring activity, cold-blooded courage, continuous readiness to sacrifice himself in the most difficult situations and in the greatest peril of his life, we, the German army High Command, feel it meet that we should press to your breast this here gong: it is the Iron Cross First Class, that means, at this hour of our imminent victory over the Allied forces, you are among the bravest of our glorious German brave. Glory O; glory O, to the bould Alpine man. *Heil!*

BLINDED by poison gas, lying among the wounded at a military hospital in Pomerania, the hero Hitler hears the unbelievable news that Germany has unconditionally surrendered to the Allies. His glory is gone. He is no more now than any other despised, defeated, utterly wretched and conquered foeman.

There is yet use for him, though, the German army decides, use for this weird, jumpy, passionate and articulate Bohemian corporal and windbag. Find something for him. Send him off to that prisoner of war camp for Russians, make him a senior screw for a few weeks, hear his eyesight is recovered, wrote a poem called 'The Blind', let him lord it over a heap of those Slav sub-humans he continually grunts on about, might perk him up. Now, these red sailor boys who have established a Soviet Republic in Munich of all places, bide our time, let's see who joins them, then we will move. Good idea, the Kaiser has abdicated so we will have our own republic based in, where? Weimar? Oh, all right, but we, the army, will run the show and we will let those damned politicians take all the stick, which is what damned politicians are for. Yes, this Communism is very attractive to lots of our chaps who, as you may imagine, are frightfully demoralised and will clutch at anything which sounds promising for the future. Get on to Mayr in Intelligence, he'll have blokes to join both left and right groups, we will soon know who proposes to do what to whom. Get on to Van Epp of the right wing mercenaries and Röhm of the general staff, we'll put down these jolly Jack Tars of this Soviet Munich with a combination of both. That way we keep an eye on things and keep our options open. Mayr says that we need some anti-Bolshie agitators to stand on soap boxes at transit camps and lay down some good old-fashioned nationalistic codswallop. Who? Yes, that sort of chap. Doesn't he get over-inflated, though, carried quite away on all that Aryan, Runic and Odic emanations rot? What? Political indoctrination and propaganda course? Consistent line of thought but with individual appeal. Yes, I see that. Oh, all right, Hitler. Czechoslovakian, is he? Oh, Austrian. Sloppy lot. Now, who can we depend on in the police? Frick, yes, Pohner, yes, and who have we at the Ministry of Justice? Gürtner. Right. Get me Pohner. Pohner? We understand that quite a lot of our chaps are forming themselves into clubs of sorts, defence leagues, ex-servicemen's associations, patriotic unions, that sort of thing. They are to be encouraged, of course. That peace treaty that the, what do they call themselves, Social Democratic Party and the other rag tag and bobtails, yes, the Republican Government, signed at Versailles, is really iniquitous. Reparations which it will take generations to pay, guilt, reduction of the army to one hundred thousand men. What? Quite. Perfectly understandable thing to say. One can sympathise. I suppose that loyalty to the Fatherland does require disloyalty to the Republic but what are these rumours of political murder gangs? Do you know of any political murder gangs? Really. Get me Frick. Frick? Pohner says that in his view there aren't enough murder gangs. Yes, we realise that he is a humorist but self-defence is one thing, murder quite another. What is needed is organisation, discipline, protection. We can't have the wrong people being murdered. Get me Gürtner. Gürtner? It is most important that our loyal former servicemen who wish, as do you and I, to see our nation restored to dignity, are allowed politically to nurture our blood and soil unintimidated by these wretched Bolshevist murder gangs. Justice may be blind but her administration must surely keep an eye on the importation of alien ruffians which are wholly at variance with our, what? Good, well keep on top of it. Get me Röhm. Roly Poly? Hello, you old sausage, trust you to stash the machine guns in a convent. Who is that amazingly pretty boy you're teaching to play the mandolin? Crazy Heines. Why is he called crazy? I see. Dear Roly Poly, do be careful. Look. You and I know it was Ludendorff who threw in the towel but it was Erzberger who signed that treacherous treaty and it is that yid Rathenau who is implementing the damned policies and we simple army officers who fought at the front are quite right to resent our treatment by these so called republican politicians. It's too shaming. Which reminds me. Though I'm sure you look divine in your political wings, Roly Poly, have you yet effectively flapped them? German Workers Party. A Beercellar? Doesn't sound too promising. A what? Instruction Officer. Sounds just the sort of title

Intelligence would dream up. No, thank you, Roly Poly, speeches are not the sort of thing that I'm giddy about hearing, even if they are wonderful and even if it's our man, our Instruction Officer, who's making them. Really? That's most impressive. He wears mufti, of course. A tailcoat. How charming. That it doesn't fit is even more charming. By all means let him be on the executive committee, by all means see that he is the party director of propaganda but do you really think it necessary to rent an office? I see. Yes. National Socialist German Workers Party? Why that name? Why socialist? Does he have pink ideas? I see. I see. Well, no, in fact I don't see. It's all too complicated for me. I'm a soldier, thank God, not a politician. All right, Roly Poly, it's very good to hear your enthusiasm and if you think that it's right and it can serve our purposes, here's what I propose we do. You may use the confidential fund for the rent and expenses and to pay our Instruction Officer but, if he continues to produce solid results he will have to resign officially and then he will be funded by other sources from the army. Can't have the military dabbling in politics, can we? What's this chap's name again? Hüttler. Is that a German name?

———

WHO ARE these running down this dim and cobbled, smoking Hunsbeck street?

Tea-time, winter, 1941, my age is nine, it is an hour or so before grubby twilight, before stumbling blackout time, when no light of any sort will shine into the city's streets; all our windows and doors are blind and barred with brown sticky paper, black curtains, sandbags and old bricks. Four figures shift niftily towards me, pelting through the sooty haze and from the far end of the street. Hear the pattering clink of bootnails nimbly striking stone. See, now, racing between the pavings, approaching me rapidly, four boys flinging to each other a rugby ball; accurately, swiftly, all along the line they flick it to and fro, fro and to, surely, safely, from finger-tips to finger-tips, left to right and right to left again and now the running boys are almost up upon me but what is that that floats and flutters from the middle of the line of lads and crumples down to the cobbles?

It is a large brown paper bag. Where has it come from?

From being lately wrapped around the loaf of bread the boys have been using as a rugby ball. Unharmed the loaf; indeed the whole crust is neither broken nor bruised as, yelping triumphantly, the puffed and laughing boys carefully stuff the bread back into its proper paper bag, one lad tucks the parcel safely under his arm and chattering home they go, these four running rugby playing Hunsbeck boys, leaving me to my silent marvelling at their glorious skill.

One may with reason think that it had been irresponsible of these young, wartime boys to put at risk a scarce and precious loaf of bread by using it in substitution for a rugger ball. So, no doubt, it had been; but irresponsibility was not what these little tykes had had in their hearts. They had wished to flirt with the swift and dextrous danger of finger-tip passing when hurtling along in a diagonal line. Drop the ball, fumble it even, knock it forward or, dread, have your pass intercepted and the opposition have the advantage and possibly may score. Tricky enough to do with a true rugby ball, this finger-tip passing, with green springing turf to go tripping along, leave alone flinging about a brown paper bag holding the week's bread while galloping down a mean street and driving down hard your bootnailed toes onto the unyielding cobblestones there.

Chances were that had they irreparably damaged the apportioned lump of weekly bread, Hunsbeckian guile and resourcefulness would very possibly have conjured up another such. Failing in that then, after a moping while, it would be back to Chemical Terrace, rightful wrath and a very thick ear. Not to be unexpected, you know, in Hunsbeck, your thick ear. It seems to me that thick ears had been handed out in Hunsbeck as a form of communication. All one's thoughts known to another in one belt round the earhole. Had one of the bold, disgracefully naughty running boys broken a leg when playing in an organised rugby match, real ball and all, on arrival home with the fractured leg in plaster, it would have been important for your mum or dad to know how you really were in yourself, the real promise of your mending wholly well and then, when they knew your true state of play, for being such a dozy pillock as to let someone break your leg in the first place you would be given a solid thick ear. One's head violently chimes, there is merciful shock which, alas, dissolves away leaving only long and aching gyp.

AIR-RAID warnings had howled less frequently at that time, nor had we been bombed for almost nine months. We did not know it then but no more bombs would be dropped on us. Indeed, the blitzkrieg bombing of England had ceased. The south of the country would later know the unimaginable fear and horror of the secret weapons with which Hitler had promised to attack and destroy us: the V1 and then the V2. Propaganda. Propaganda.

The buzzbomb first, the loud, clattering pilotless plane loaded with one ton of high explosive. If the clatter stopped, your number could well be up; if the racket continued away then someone else might win first prize.

Other than at the cinema I neither saw nor heard one but my old Daddy had seen a couple. 'Obscene, Peter,' he had said to me, slowly shaking his head, his face sad and angry, 'obscene.'

Silent, though, the V2 rockets when they came. An immense ripping noise immediately before their one ton of hideous destruction landed and burst had been the only sound that they had made. Many, many thousands of people were killed by them, more injured and many more shocked and terrified.

When measured in the scale of the avalanches of fires and masonry that had been the lot by day and night of London and many other cities and towns, the little that we had endured at Hunsbeck had been no more than a pea shot from its shooter. We had been given a hint of the plot; no more; it would serve.

We now know what many of us in England then had not fully realised, as the nine months of continuous blitzkrieg bombings ceased: even one more month or so of German bombing would have surely cracked us. The inevitable deadening of constant fatigue had made impossible the ability to resist in man or machine or building; we had been close to goners that time in the summer of 1941 when Hitler had decided rather to turn his full attention towards Russia and Uncle Joe Stalin.

———————

'JOE STALIN smokes a pipe and wears a taxi driver's hat', repeat, we sang to the tune of 'The Battle Hymn of the Republic', in celebration of the appearance on our side of Josef Djzugashvili, alias Coba, alias Stalin, the former seminarian, revolutionary, gaolbird, exile in the Siberian gulags of the Tsar, token plebeian in Lenin's middle-class, intellectual, Bolshevik ruling élite; a five-foot-three-inch, hard-drinking, scurrilous little foreigner from the Holy Kingdom of Georgia in the Northern Orient, now Ruler of All the Russias.

It is 1941, the Nazis are twenty miles away from us, twenty miles made of water that we call the English Channel, our last and blessed barrier to the expansion of the Third Reich. We have formed an alliance with Russia and the ruthless, secret and implacable terror of Stalin. Hitler has turned away from us and has hurled his people at Stalin and Russia. Hitler and Germany have met their match.

Most of that historic spring and summer my mother, sister and I had lived either close to where Captain Pat, my father was happily doing his unexpected bit for the war effort, or out with Wilf and Dee at lovely hillocky Starsbottom. Slowly my sister was learning to live with her asthma. Every evening my mother would hold a large spoon filled with almond oil over the flame from a candle; when the sweet oil had been warmed, Mummy would ripple her fingers in it and then carefully, firmly, she would massage the unction onto my sister's scalp, all the while talking or singing softly to her. Slowly, slowly, dark and curly my sister's hair began to grow again.

Illusory, of course, but out in rural Yorkshire during those longer, brighter spring and summer days there had seemed to me to be more eggs and butter than we had known back in the city. Meat and sugar, too, tea and peace and light, lemonade, sunshine and no fear at all to gnaw into my guts as I hopped upon the stepping stones to cross the river running round the ruins of the old abbey there, assuming as I did my various roles of Robin or Sir Yvain or the marvellous Merlin.

STAND ON these stones and see the bulging waters suck and bubble around them. Watch the small winged creatures fly and skim along the stretching, dimpled grey and blue skin of the living river. Hear the plops and splashes and the stony groans as the endless water roams along its course. Hop onto the next stone, don't step where it is green, now, step where it is dark. Step where it is green, your foot will slip, slide and you will tumble yet again into the river; no, step onto the dark of the stone, there you will perch safely.

Hop. All's well.

Cool this sweet breeze as I stand on a stepping stone in the river's middle to gaze up at the great black arching silence of the forsaken abbey.

Did Friar Michael Tuck say Mass here in the long long ago? Is this where he broke bread with his brother monks, seated at the long refectory table? Where he sang hymns, where he prayed, where he dug for spuds? Did that wonderful barney that he had had with the abbot happen right here? Tuck had been quite right, you know, and Daddy agrees; that abbot had been a traitor to Jesus and not his disciple, going around grabbing money and goods and land, even homes, from the poor. Why, Jesus would have given them the shirt off his back and would then have washed their feet, just as that sweet lady who had done such an awful lot of sinning had washed His poor feet, and with her tears.

That abbot had been a bloody hypocrite, yes, hypocrite. It would have been worth half my sweet ration to see Friar Tuck bump the bugger with his big fat belly and knock him arse over tip.

Hop.

Huge the building looms above me now; massive, eerie, quiet. Am I frightened? Yes, a bit. 'Art freckened, you daft little bastard?' Wilf had said to me after he had piloted me safely across the river by way of the stepping stones and seen me flinch a little before wandering with him through this huge and silent ruin. To be freckened was to be frightened in Wilf's way of speaking and Wilf's way of speaking was ripe and deep and blunt and full of new words with old meanings. Also, he was always what you and I might think as being rude to almost everyone but no one seemed to mind a bit. Wilf was a very big man indeed, who seemed to me to be made of iron and whose hands were the size of shovels. Wilf and his wife, Dee, were friends of my parents and it was at a pub in which they owned an interest, call it the White Hind, that we were staying.

'There's nowt to be freckened of, you gormless little sod, there's only the spirits of the dead lives here now and they couldn't knock the skin off a rice pudding.'

Perhaps, Wilf, perhaps, but looking up from my stepping stone, through the grass on the bank and the leaves on the trees, this ancient place with its wide and empty windows, its doors all gone and stripped of its roof, seems an ideal spot for specially nasty spirits of the dead and, whatever of rice puddings, it is the skin I live in that they might wish to knock off and, yes, I am a bit freckened. Just a bit.

Not frightened as I had been during the blackouts of the

previous winter in Hunsbeck. Blackout. That is what lives on in my mind; the complete blacking out of much of our sentient life for many, many months. The darkness which Shakespeare tells us that the blind do see, the deep necessary darks we had made of our streets and roads and paths, the sealing in of all light from our houses and buildings, so that no brightness would glint in the target sights of the German bombers hunting in the air above us, a darkness so thick that one had felt it could be grabbed in handfuls.

Every evening at a set time my father and mother had arranged to speak to one another on the telephone. We had been among the many in Hunsbeck who at that time had owned no telephone and so for my Mum to have her nightly chunter with my old Pop, war worker, had meant for her a two-hundred-yard rambling, stumbling, bumping trek through the filthy darkness of the blackout, groping towards the nearest telephone booth which had stood hard by where the clattering, darkened tramcars made a stop. I had accompanied my mother on many of these nifty jaunts and tell you that at times we had been terrified, often we really had clung to each other; at times we had been plainly lost, at other times we found ourselves falling flat on our faces; often it had been painful, often it had been funny, always it had been black as pitch as, at first, we had shuffled sideways, our fingers feeling out for familiar walls, window-ledges, doors, fences, moving, as all who had walked out of doors during those early winter blackouts of the war had moved, falteringly, timorously, sensing, perhaps, what young mankind had known on moonless nights before the discovery and conservation of fire.

One night, when we had blundered off course, we found ourselves, as it were, with one foot on the pathway and one foot on the cobbles. This happy accident proved to be our answer to the bruising difficulties of blind navigation. From then on we had trudged lopsidedly to the chuckling, reassuring voice of Daddy, in bobbing line astern, taking it in turns to be the one in front, but always with the right foot on the cobble, the left foot on the kerb.

When the iron drain on the kerbside had been reached, it was then slowly, slowly, gently feel out for the unlit lamp-post standing there, for we had not wanted to walk into that bloody thing again, feel with your feet where the pavement turns left, got it, well, then, left foot on the kerb, right foot on the cobbles till you reach the sandbags, here we cross the street, there is a row of cobbles in a regular line which leads right to the opposite path, you can feel them by carefully juddering your heel across their surfaces, that's the way, now, right foot on the kerb, left foot on the cobbles until you meet the iron drain and the next unlit lamp-post.

Thus, by kerb and cobble, by bollard or post or stanchion or wall or window or rail or fence or drain or sandbag, in the blackout times of the Second World War we feelingly went our ways.

Alas, all too many men, women and children had walked into unlit lamp-posts and worse during those first blacked-out months. The daily rate for deaths, accidentally caused by the blackout, ran to dozens. Our safety precautions were killing more citizens than enemy bombs had thus far succeeded in doing. But that would change.

One time, when travelling to the north of the city to stay with friends, the bus that my mother and I were on was running very late, delayed by the inevitable snarls and jams of traffic on wartime roads. The idea had been to get there before nightfall, before blackout time, but now here we were in the centre of the city and night was falling quickly. Not that I cared very much. Most of us wartime children in England had soon become used to terror of the dark, to loss, to separation, to alienation, to restriction, to alarm. Some of us, perhaps quite a lot of us, were beginning to find some of quite a lot of this here war lark to be really quite exciting and, any road, how bad could it be sitting next to your lovely Mum on the front seats of the left-hand row of the lower deck of a warm bus, facing the big window which let you peer at the way that the bus was rolling, and pretending to be the driver? You could see the real driver in his cabin just above you on the right and when he tugged his levers to change gear then I tugged mine, and when he two-handedly heaved his big wheel round to the left or the right, then I hauled mine round in a similarly grand manner.

What I hadn't anticipated was the driver braking so suddenly and so heavily.

The passengers all pitched forward, my mother grabbed me, and then I heard a loud crack and a deep, heavy thud. Crushed sideways into the window ahead of me was a man's face. Some of his body I could see too, and an arm that seemed to stretch sideways from under his chin. For a long minute he stayed there and bright blood dashed against the window in red spurts. Then he was gone; leaving on the window only a long dark bloody smear. Beetroot juice came to mind.

Hunsbeck had been quite enough to contend with, thank you, let alone blackouts and their unhappy consequences. For openers there had been the lingo. In place of you or your or yours, thee, thy, thou or thine had been sometimes familiarly and popularly used in some parts of northern England when I was young. They may use the terms still. In Hunsbeck, when addressing another, they had used nothing but. That and a choice and pronunciation of words that at first seemed to me to be incomprehensible. 'Tha wet? Wot art t'up to, tha rats' knackers? See thissen off or tha'lt 'ave me clog terplug th'arsole up wi'.' Thou what? What art thou up to, thou rats' knackers? See thyself off or thou shalt have my clog to plug thy arsehole up with.

The distinguished writer handsome, haunted W. Hall, a fellow Hunsbeckian, and I can, do and, yes, will, speak to each other in Hunsbeck *patois*. Of course, we only do this when in the company of souls who find it difficult to believe that such base coinage could ever have been a common currency of speech. One time, in a properly staid and conservative gentlemen's club in London, we gave to an assembly of members our tuneful duet of a revered Hunsbeck ditty, 'Weer orl darn int selleroil wert muck slats up t'winnders'. We are all down in the cellar hole where the dirt boards up the windows. One gentleman member who had politely endured our performance, felt moved enough to remark that he was sure that he had heard the song before, sung by Africans in the Leslie Banks film *Sanders of the River*.

Then there had been the business of my neat black shoes.

The days and weeks of my early explorations in darkest Hunsbeck had revealed to me hosts of ways and wonders. Long strings of alleys called ginnels which had threaded themselves between warehouses and mills and factories, over railway lines, across canals, rambling down to the river, winding behind pubs, shops, the library and leading to the broad dark arches which let one through to the centre of the city.

Throngs of boys, my own age or younger or older, tumbled, ran and whooped their ways through these fascinating labyrinths. Steel hoops were bowled along, steered and propelled by metal hooks. A bicycle with no tyres provided three or even four scamps with a delightful, rickety, bucking vehicle. One roller skate for each lad had seemed to be the standard issue and hadn't they just stamped and rolled along in fine careers? Hadn't they leapt, pirouetted and then landed to skid along amazingly on one hot-wheeled wobbling skate?

These, indeed, had been paths for me willingly to roam and investigate; splendid sports in which to play my part and welcome they had made me, those rough, tough Hunsbeck boys, my differences of manner and speech giving them only matter for rough-tongued chiding; hard and rowdy but not cruel.

My treatment by the neighbour boys, in those early Hunsbeck days, had often been alarming, often strange to me, often I had been the butt of their pranks and jokes and always they had played to hard and boisterous limits but no one had been minded to thump me more than I had deserved; nor had I been bullied or tormented and, in time, wearing my rightfully got thick ears proudly and carrying in my bearing the strut and glow of a boy who had been named the Tooler by his fellows, I had soon learned that any attempt to throw one's puny weight about was a serious mistake. In Hunsbeck the life of a bully had been precious short. Ginnels had been dangerous roads to travel if you enjoyed being a thug.

The most serious barrier to my entry into this society of ragged-arsed tykes had been my neat and polished small black shoes. 'Th'art shod like a fucking bally dancer,' had been the opinion expressed to me through a spokesman for the heap. Their point had been plainly made and easily understood. Thick, hobnailed boots had been the wear for ginnel lads. Miners' boots, donkeymen's boots, dads' cast-off boots, patched, cobbled and thickly nailed jobs but, most certainly, boots. Some had worn clogs. Leather clogs, wooden clogs, clogs with soles metal as horseshoes. They had hopscotched in their clogs and boots, they had shimmied up down pipes; rugby and cricket and tig they had played in their boots and clogs; they had skipped and sprinted and tiptoed in their traditional footwear and, naturally, they had been loath to admit into their brotherhood one who was shod like a fucking bally dancer.

I had owned no boots, nor clogs, but I did have a pair of light plimsolls. Pumps, we called them, and those I had worn in the slow days of watchful, quizzical, tweaking and gradual admittance of me and my pumps into their society. Painful, mind you, for a trotter so lightly encased when, during a game of, say, pig in the middle, a coal heaver's clog comes grinding down onto the toes. One learned to be nimble. And nimble now am I as I hop across the water and safely land on the next stepping stone.

Hop.

Sweet Jesus, oh but this old abbey is bare and black and massive and towers above me hugely up into the sky. Wide it is, too, wide and ranging and with darkness tumbling into its many roofless rooms and nooks and chapels and corridors.

Wilf says that the first monks to eat meat every day had lived here. That in the first wall you meet as you enter into the abbey there is a door that leads you into the huge room where the sides of the beef and the boar and the venison had been skinned and gutted and seasoned and cooked.

Be that as it may, Wilf, be that as it may, but where is the portcullis? Surely no mighty building from the long ago of any note could be without a portcullis? A portcullis was an altogether splendid thing. A great heavy iron grille with terrible spikes sticking out from its grating and its base. It had blocked the gateway into castles, fortresses, palaces and, surely, abbeys. It could be raised or lowered to admit or bar. It could be dropped suddenly and frightfully in times of danger as witness Sir Yvain on the day that he had ridden into a place of peril all debonair and gallant, easily riding his trotting charger, knowing he wore the magic ring that he could twist to make himself invisible.

It must still have been an awful shock to him when that dirty great portcullis had come crashing down, chopping his poor horse in half. When that portcullis had whistled down, it had even grazed Sir Yvain's hair and backplate but had not harmed him at all. It had harmed his horse, though, the portcullis had gone straight through the brute and had chopped it neatly in half. Half the animal was inside the castle and half of it was outside. The head, neck, breast and forelegs were on one side of the portcullis, while the backlegs, arse and tail were on the other. Sir Yvain had, of course, twisted his ring and vanished but the two halves of the horse hadn't. Even days later, when the fuss was all over, after the portcullis had been raised, the two parts of the horse had still stood there. You could see right through its middle and, strangest of all, it was still alive.

Perhaps Merlin glued it together and sent it off scampering entirely, I forget. One of my strongest memories, though, from all the fiction that I had read or heard at that time during the war when I was nine or so, is the story of the fate of Sir Yvain's horse.

One time, when riding in a Paris ascenseur and in the company of two pretty ladies, the chimes of midnight having sounded, it had been mooted a fine notion to ascend to an apartment owned by one of the young women and there, that merry night, to carry on whatever it was that we were celebrating. The ascenseur was a belle époque number: criss-cross metal accordion doors, wrought-iron flourishes all twirls and loops and lilies, polished mahogany, shining brightwork and with matching artwork at every floor to accord with the arrival or departure of this fine, art-nouveau ascenseur. It was also asthmatic, wheezing, arthritic, reluctant, shaky, slow and, of course, old.

We three passengers, chirruping blithely of this or that and the price of turnips; young, flushed, vigorous and on the razzle, had been dismayed to discover that our ancient, utilitarian work of art was no longer groaning inchingly upwards but had, in fact, quite given up the ghost, had ceased these labours up and down and had stopped. Stopped unbudgingly to hang there dangling, jammed between one floor and the adorned door of our destination.

Yes, to be sure, we had pressed all the buttons provided, we had bellowed and stamped and pleaded and raved; we had rattled and called up, we had rattled and called down, but no present occupiers in the apartments had heard or heeded our prayers; no fish-eyed concierge on the ground floor, usually so alert to who comes and who goes through the doors of a Parisian apartment block, had stirred a feather behind his or her peephole to answer our supplications.

Perhaps all the apartments had been soundproofed, sound-proofed particularly against the racket made by this slamming, aching and decrepit old elevator; perhaps the snooping concierge had swallowed a pailful of boozie rouge and lay in untroubled, rosy, alcoholic coma. Who knows?

What had certainly been made known to us was that an hour and more sitting on the floor of a small and cramped, stuck ascenseur, distress signals ignored, pressed down by a leaden heat inducing irritation and sweat, an evaporation of cheerful banter, a diminishing supply of cigarettes and the slow, sure approach of cold sobriety, had earned from we threesome a response less frolicsome than had been our earlier wont, less abandoned, sensuous and lightsome; more glum, more grumpy, more bad-humoured even, tetchy, more cabined, cribbed, confined, more inclined to resent our predicament and its comfortless absurdity.

Now, one of my fair companions hailed from Berchtesgarden, yes, Berchtesgarden, and perhaps, I fancy, a little something in the ether there may have permeated into her through her pores because, of a sudden, up she stood and with wide blue eyes glaring down at me where I lolled harmlessly puffing a remainder dog-end on the squeezing deck, she had loudly croaked out at me, 'Peter, you are supposed to be a man. Do something!'

Those of you who have ridden in one such antique, French ascenseur will know that the ornate box you stand in for your journey has no roof. Indeed, all above you is the chute provided for the vehicle's progress as it wobbles up and down or not. That and huge heavy loops of greasy black steel cable which, when you are happily moving, writhe and coil about both above and on either side of the cabin. Also, I had spotted, there was one particularly thick cluster of plaited grease and wire which hung immediately over the centre of our small, suspended trap and which seemed to have extensions from it stretching to the far corners of the box. Perhaps this was the cord which held our collective weight, the bond on which we helplessly dangled, a bond, moreover, whose old strands might even now be frayed and, from the exhaustion of a lifetime of labours, be snapping one by one. 'Yes, my Fräulein,' I said, I fancy, 'you are quite right. I am a man and faint heart never fucked a pig. Please, both of you, make backs.'

Assisted by this stern Brünnhilde and by our other friend, the dark-haired beauty, now sobbing noisily, with much writhing and crouching and effortful grunting, with a foot on a buttock and the other on a spine, with a heave and a ho, and a foot on a shoulder and the other on a face, a little leap from me and I had grabbed two handfuls of the stretching greasy pole. A further, desperate pull and up there I was, my arms and legs wrapped tightly round the creaking strands of an oily cable.

'Go on!' said a voice.

'Boo hoo,' said another and on and up I somehow went.

A little purchase on one side of the shaft, a little more from the other, all the while hugging and clasping the slipping, sliding wires. A few frantic minutes later and my spidering ended. There, feet only from where I clung and swung, was the door to the ascenseur which let into it from the floor above.

A swing and a kick but the door moved not an inch. A swinging, heaving, two footed stamping kick and the door budged not at all. Nor did anyone answer my baying and beseeching.

Hope yet, though, for it was not all door, no, the topmost quarter was a grille.

Tug, tug, shove and scramble and there, opposite my face, was a fancy, art-nouveau, beautifully tooled metal grille. There was a lily in the middle and leaves and branches sloping down from the flower until they met, on either side, two splendidly wrought twirls. Through that grille there was escape and a lighted landing.

Between the sharp leaves and the twirls there was surely room enough for one slim as me to slither through. My feet and legs went through first, I the while hanging on with my hands to the swaying, greased cable, and with much shoving, ripping and wriggling my bottom followed hard upon.

It was time to gulp a big breath and so, with half of me dangling outside the grille and the other half of me inside, grabbing and grunting, I rested my belly for a brief second on the sharp branches and the pointed leaves, the bulging twirl grinding into the base of my ribcage.

Then it was that the old ascenseur jolted into unexpected life and the cabin began to judder slowly upwards.

A vision of Sir Yvain's horse came neighing into my mind and whether I levitated or floated or changed shape as mercury might, I have no fair recollection. What I do recall is a blood rush of panic and a determined wish not to be ripped into halves by a rising ascenseur and in the next instant I found myself lying on the landing staring wildly at a fancy grille on which was hanging a lot of my trousers, some of my leg, considerable stretches of my jacket and shirt, a stripe of skin from my neck and a hank of hair from my head.

Otherwise I was intact.

Nor had my frenzied haste been necessary. The lift had risen up only a foot or so and then had stayed stuck again, leaving the ladies still trapped. Some old neurone in the mechanism of the quaint and ancient device may have prompted a reflexive convulsion which had caused it to lurch up a notch. That was all.

Happily I found the right apartment door on which to hammer. To wake the maid who alerted the concierge who telephoned the superintendent who summoned the fire brigade who called the engineers and, came first light, the joint was milling with boiler suits, *gendarmerie*, brass helmets, dressing gowns and dapper anxious men waving their arms and bellowing.

The maid and I stuffed a shopping bag with champagne, bottled water, cigarettes and paper hankies, tied a length of twine to it, rammed it through the grille where bits of me were still adhering and lowered it to the unfortunate prisoners still stifling down below.

No door to the ascenseur could be opened unless the ascenseur had reached its appropriate slot and though for my money a tap or two with a *pompier*'s chopper would have turned the trick nicely, it was decided to winch the whole issue up from the top of the building. This would take an hour or two I was told and so I limped around to my own pad, which was a couple of hundred yards or so away, dunked myself in a soapy tub, dabbed on a little iodine, jumped into fresh gear, swallowed a reviving bottle of beer and then tottered back to bedlam in the avenue.

Winching was still going on, went on for quite a while, slowly on and on with starts and stops, much chatter, commands, counter-commands and howled reassurance to the unfortunate ladies drooping down below.

Eventually it was all over: the cabin clicked into its proper slot, the door opened to applause from sundry, and out onto the jammed landing crept Brünnhilde and Niobe.

Niobe was beyond all comforting and was led gibbering into the apartment. But not Brünnhilde. Tired, unhappy, crumpled Brünnhilde, who had breakfasted on tobacco, champagne and deep resentment, fixed comparatively fresh me with her best, beady and Berchtesgaden look; then, from down deep within herself, she growled, 'So. You escaped and left us to suffer. How do you propose to explain yourself?'

How indeed, my sweet, dear Fräulein, how indeed?

Hop. Almost there. A willow weeps into the river here and hides away the ruins from my eyes. This stone is big and bulks up way above the water's flow so on it I will sit a while and think about the incendiary bomb.

Roly had spotted it. A slim grey metal bulby tube with what seemed to be a darker-coloured handle to it ending in a round knob. It was lying on the edge of the waste ground, beyond where the ginnel over the railway led out. Roly didn't know what it was, nor I or Hooky and Willis thought it was an American baseball bat. He had seen them at the pictures.

I picked it up and though it was fairly heavy it was easy enough to lift and seemed to me to be about twice the weight of a grown-up's cricket bat. Still, 'Finders keepers, losers weepers', Roly had seen it first so it was rightly his; but we took it in turns to carry it as we sauntered through the ginnel into the broad street where the shops are, looking for other young tigers who might like to take a look at our discovery. Roly's discovery.

It was just outside the poulterer's where Hooky sat down with the tin club between his knees and began trying to twist the roundy knob. Out of the poultry shop came a young man wearing blue workman's overalls and carrying a skinned rabbit wrapped round with white greaseproof paper. He knelt down beside Hooky, put his parcel down on the pavement, took hold of our find with two hands and said, 'Piss off lads it's a bomb.'

Then he took the bomb into the middle of the cobbled road, placed it down, returned to the shop, came out again in seconds, joined by the poulterer, both bearing sandbags, and the two of them put the sandbags over the bomb. They both then repeated their errand over and over until the bomb lay under a mound of sandbags.

Their deed done, the workman looked at the poulterer and said, 'Tha'd best finned a bobby or summat, tell im wotsup. Weers me fucking rabbit?' Thou would'st best find a policeman or suchlike and tell him what has gone on. Where is my fucking rabbit?

We were minding his rabbit. No one was going to touch that man's rabbit. We would kill anyone who tried to nick his rabbit.

'It's 'ere, mister,' Hooky said, handing the man his parcel, but he was too shy and felt too daft to look that brave man in the eye.

INCENDIARY BOMB WITH EXPLOSIVE NOSE (IBEN)

When the bomb lands the striker fires the detonator which ignites both the cap and the flash-train. The flash from the cap fires the main incendiary filling which eventually ignites the inflammable alloy case of the incendiary unit. Meanwhile the flash-train sets off the time fuse. This burns slowly for up to seven minutes, and then fires a second detonator which detonates the main explosive charge. The main explosive charge is carried in a steel container which bursts into many fragments when the charge detonates. The thin metal nose cover is not always found on the bomb.

Hop.

Make me brave as Yvain, please, for he is my man.

Evainne in some books; sometimes Evan, sometimes a son of Morgan Le Fay, sometimes not. In one Arthur book, written by a lady, with coloured, cissy illustrations, he doesn't even get a mention. Sir Yvain is my man, though, my secret man really for not many boys in England can know about Sir Yvain.

Mrs Pender has told me all about Sir Yvain, in his gold and in his green. Tutankhamen's spoon, too, I have learned about. And Mrs Pender has often let me hold that wonderfully decorated gilded box that a soldier or a sailor could keep his proud possessions in.

Mrs Pender is old and nice and very tall. Mrs Pender keeps a boarding house and is French really, but she married an Irishman a long time ago. He was killed in Ireland during the Rebellion and her son was killed in France during the Great War. Daddy says that there were other women in Ireland at that time who had lost both a husband and a son, but that in their cases it was mostly the boy who had died in Ireland and the da who had been killed in France.

They were both heroes: soldiers who had died in battle.

The gilded box had belonged to her son. It had been given to him by a princess who had had a number of them made to give to soldiers and sailors for their precious objects: cigarettes and money and watches and collar studs.

Mrs Pender has told me all about the French story of King Arthur and of the old Welsh story of King Arthur. Of Merlin, of Sir Yvain, of Lancelot and Galahad and Gawaine, of Bors, Lot, Lucan, Pellinore; of the Lady Luned, of Guinevere, and of Morgan Le Fay, of Bran the Blessed and Efnissien and Matholuch; of Loki and Thor, of Weiland, Sigurd and Siegfried; of Tara, of the Land of the Giants, of the Island of the Mighty, the Purple City, Tir nan Og and of Middle Earth.

Tutankhamen's spoon used to be kept in the drawer of a table standing in front of the fire in her sitting room. The gilded box lies in her desk where the photographs of her husband and her son stand. Mrs Pender must have hundreds of books, and they stand in bookshelves that rise right up to the ceiling. Digs are very important to my father and he says that there are no better digs than Mrs Pender's. I agree with him. We haven't seen her for a long while, now; and I miss her and the stories.

We would sit on her sofa, before us on a small table would be ginger beer in stone bottles or Tizer or American Cream Soda and always there would be Turkish Delight or milk chocolate or liquorice allsorts. Munching and swigging I would sit next to her listening to her read or tell me great stories of ancient Europe, Ireland and Britain, sometimes so lost was I in these amazing yarns that I would forget to swig or munch. Often Mrs Pender would get a book which had a picture in it of the scene that she was describing. Always Mrs Pender found the book straight away and if the book was shelved up high she had a long thick black pole which somehow opened up into a ladder, and on this she would clamber up and down easily and lightly.

The illustrations of Sir Yvain killing the evil giant and rescuing the Lady Luned, who is about to be burned alive for treason, are wonderful and so is the one of Yvain watching his lion disembowel the wicked Seneschal who had falsely accused Luned.

'We bring monsters to our fireside and make them our pets, don't we, Peter?'

The time that I broke Tutankhamen's spoon, though, had really put the heart across me. It was small and black, very black, thin as eggshell and very, very fragile. I had often been allowed to look at it, sitting in its drawer under the table cover. Sometimes, after vowing to be specially careful, I had been allowed to hold it, Tutankhamen's spoon. On this day, however, there being not a soul about, not only was I going to look at the ancient treasure, I was going to pick it up and examine it carefully.

I had been much younger, of course, but I had always felt a strange, nervous thrill when the drawer pulled out and there was the fine, black, small spoon that Tutankhamen had used when he ate his boiled egg.

Honestly, I picked it up and held it as gently as I could. All I wanted to do was carry it carefully across the room, hold it up to the window light and see if it was transparent. Truly. I don't know how I didn't see the stool as I bumped into it but I never shall forget the spoon as it fell from my hands on to the floorboards by the window and there snapped in half.

Tutankhamen's spoon in bits.

All I could think of to do was to hide the pieces of the spoon under the paper which lined its drawer, and then I knew that I could either run away and never be found, stick my head in the gas oven and there die, as many people we heard about had done, or, mercy, own up. Make a clean breast of it, as Mummy says.

The gas oven is beyond me, anyway I am not allowed to touch it. There is nothing to stop me running away but it is getting dark. Obviously, the best thing is to leave the spoon hidden where it is and hope that nobody notices anything.

That is what I did but all night I was sorry and troubled. Tutankhamen's spoon was a rare and wonderful object to me and all the owning up in the world would not mend the broken thing.

The following morning, heartbroken and shaking, holding my mother's hand, I had sobbed out to Mrs Pender the story of my crime.

Well, we know now that it had only been a steel teaspoon that had fallen into the fire one day, had stayed in the fire until it was burned into a black crisp, had been found by Mrs Pender in the cold ashes and who, the spoon being strange and quaint, had kept it in her table drawer, calling it in her serious, twinkle-eyed way, Tutankhamen's spoon.

The treasure box had been real enough, the books and stories, of course, and now that I am more grown-up, I think I understand the point of pretending that the spoon had once belonged to that great, Ancient Egyptian Pharaoh, but my soul had sorely grieved that time when I believed that I had broken Tutankhamen's spoon, and I never shall forget it.

It would be very nice to see Mrs Pender again, though. Maybe when this bloody war is over; when we shall go racing again.

Hop.

One more step, I shall be across the river and shall stand alone on the streaming bank under the gloomy looming abbey.

My mother may well be looking for me, often is, often says I'm always missing, always off somewhere, always up to something, always where I shouldn't be rarely where I should. She has spent a lot of time in the last few months trying to teach me my arithmetic tables. Some are quite easy but when it comes to the sevens, eights and nines I am hopeless. It's said that the schools may open again next year. Let's see: other than my brief time among the strange pagans at Lossborough, it will be over two years since I saw the inside of a school. My mother does her best, trying to keep me up to scratch, but I think it's fairly pointless. She has had more success with some of our neighbours in Hunsbeck. Quite a lot of the older ones don't know how to read or write and my mother is often reading or writing letters for them, filling in forms for them, showing them how not to be bullied by the women handing out ration books or clothing coupons and even teaching some of them how to use the telephone, many of them have never used one before. If someone feels unwell, Mummy always tells them if they should see a doctor or not. Indeed, the folk in Peartree Lane have taken a great liking to my mother for she is at all times helpful, always bustling about with a word to pass with them about this or t'other and she always keeps a crust of bread for the coalman's horse.

Constance Jane Eliot Ferguson in the grim and wartime days at Hunsbeck in 1941. Aye, and what of pretty wee Constance Jeanie, though? No crimson tipped flowers for her among the reeky cobblestones. Not too many bonny blue banknotes, either, to provide her with all comfort and high distinction. Daddy, Patricia and me, we were her riches and her fame. Perhaps not quite what as a younger woman she had had in mind, but we were what life had handed out to her and she gave to us all the love that she owned.

Prior to her unfortunately happy encounter with Daddy, Constance Jane had been the loving fancy of a jazz-band singer. A crooner. My little Mum had fancied him, too, but had continued to work at a hospital for incurables in the west of England and so could be with Tonsils only during her holidays, which were few, so Tonsils used to warble up west quite a bit and a little touch of his stardust fell on my mother's foot. Quite a fizz had run through the hospital staff, some of it even delighting a few of her dying charges.

Now, I never saw my mother in a uniform so it cannot have started there, but was there anything more sinfully wholesome than your nursie in the days when she was fair iced with shining starch, a headdress prim and saucy, stockings of silky black, with a little clock on upside down ticking over her tit, not permitted to run except in cases of haemorrhage or fire, writhing about something merciless and feeling your pulse?

Nursecake, my old Daddy. Certainly. Bite it.

The vagabond lover had shown my old Mum a way of life to which she could very easily have become accustomed. The trouble was that although Tonsils had remained keen, wee Jeanie's commitment had dulled. Tonsils would have sussed that, a light has gone out, it seems, and it won't come back on again. There is joy no more in simple tangible affection and it is a slow shock.

The sweet singer put away his banjo, returned to the city, cleared his throat, and in pubs and clubs and cafés, on records and on the air-waves of the wireless, he crooned out his moony tunes to ears and hearts more sentimentally responsive than had been wee Constance Jeanie's.

Clambering out of bed to do a midnight gig in 1941, a German bomb had dropped on his head and that had put an end to his melody.

It was said of Hunsbeck that there the crows flew backwards to keep the shit out of their eyes, and my mother took up her scrubbing brush and bucket to toil with our neighbours at the ceaseless task of banishing from our bodies, clothes and homes the visit of industrial filth.

Hop.

Here I am now among the black, broken, silent stones; walking quietly along the tumbled passageways; ahead of me the church tower darkens out the sky but there is no fear in me, only wonder that this mighty and so sacred place should be so ruined and so deserted.

A king had come here with his knights. They had tethered their horses to the confessionals; they had cooked their food in the lady chapel; they had fastened their falcons to the golden crosses; they had pissed in the holy water; the king had ordered his bed to be made on the altar and all through the night he had snored there; they had killed all the monks, sold all the nuns, plundered the abbey of its treasures and had then destroyed and ruined it utterly.

All these many hundreds of years and few can have minded this desolate place. Its towers remain broken, its great arches wrecked, and only I it seems to stand and gaze among this vast black hulk of stones; nor question why at all but accept that in our burning cities still stand the gaunt wreckages of buildings, of castle or palace or church or home, somehow standing upright after all around them has been destroyed. We see it by day and by night now in England; we see it after it has happened, some of us; we look at its picture practically every day; on the newsreel, in the newspaper, the comic even. 'Oh, my *Dandy* and my *Beano* long ago!'

The man who had ordered this destruction of life and lands and cities had been pictured in our comic books of the time as a raving buffoon. Hitler wore jackboots, had a big arse covered in breeches, a silly face, had a comical tash, a flopping forelock, sweated, shouted and swore. Goering was always drawn as a great pudding in an overcoat jangling with medals. Hermann was a guinea a minute to me, alongside Desperate Dan and Lord Snooty, but not Hitler. Couldn't see the joke, I suppose; still can't.

Hitler must die. Secret Agent O'Toole, codename Merlin, badly shot in the leg, the wound bandaged by my snotty hanky, not dismayed, we delivered the codes to the hollow tree in the village, got spotted, shot, escaped, made our painful way to the deserted abbey, where at midnight under a full moon, Hitler will speak.

We shall deliver our people from war and suffering and bring peace to them by shooting this evil man.

Hitler cannot know that our codes had broken his codes and we know that exactly at midnight, after the torchlight procession, Hitler will stand before the altar to make his oration. Then we shall bag him.

From our secret perch on the top of this wall, which we have climbed and not counted the agony this caused our wound, there will be the perfect spot to get Hitler in the range of these exploding bullets from our gun, to get him in our telescopic sight, and then as he begins his speech, to shoot him in the face.

'Dah-dah-dah-daaah! You are to come in for your tea, you blue-eyed little bastard.'

It's Wilf. He would know where I had got to. He's come for me.

'Dah-dah-dah-daaah! Don't climb down, lad, jump, break your fucking neck, we'd have one less to water and feed. Jump. Dah-dah dah-daaah! That's Beethoven, that is, cloth ears, he's set the Morse code to music has fucking Beethoven, that's the V for Victory sound, that is. Three dots and a dash. Dah-dah-dah-daaah! Winston Churchill's ordered it to be played on the wireless every time it's switched on and already it's driving me crackers. You switch on the wireless hoping to hear something pleasant like that bastard who pasted your bowling all over the park has been crushed by a tractor, and what do you get your lugs plugged up with? Dah-dah-dah-daaah! It makes you weep. Go on, you first over the stones and fall in you gormless young melt there'll be one less to piss in the po. V for Victory, I should cocoa. It'll be a while yet I reckon but Churchill says that everybody who's fighting the Germans has to chalk up on walls the V for Victory sign. Chalk it up on my walls and I'll break some bastard's back, next he'd be chalking up "Free Beer". We're also told to make a V with two fingers of our right hand and then to jerk the arm up in a salute. That's the Victory sign, says Churchill, and we are all to make it. Well, it may mean "Victory" to Churchill and lots of others, but here in Yorkshire we've been making that sign for centuries, bloody centuries, and it doesn't mean "Victory" up here, up here it means "Fuck you and your relatives in Bradford!" Wash your face and hands you horrible little toad, then get in to your mammy and your daddy, they've been looking for you, tell them you've been at church with me, then make the V sign, you'll be very popular.'

⸻

MANY, MANY years later, one day, due to play in a game of cricket, being not very far from Starsbottom, the match being a forty-over job starting at 2 p.m., found three team-mates and me, on a sunny summer's morning, with options. We could either spend a couple of hours having a net or we could take a jaunt. Two of us were playing well enough, two of us were beyond repair, so we settled on a spin around local parts familiar to me and off we rolled in my roomy motor car.

A great bowl of high, rocky woodland rims around a village, a small bridge over a river, and the great, silent, abbey ruins. Hidden from all sight around until the small curving road lets you into its light. A secret, lovely, sacred place.

To the broad miles of smoking purple Yorkshire moorlands next, a few miles away. To stand on a height and stare down at this immense stretch of wild colour. To wander along a flat track through the moor, among horned sheep, as around us a wilderness of thistle and heather hugely sways. To remark how, when the hard rain tumbles, the wind axes in from the east and thick mist admits only a sight of the tearing scrag immediately around you, it is no place to be without a hat. To cricket.

Oliver. Yorkshire. 1952

Me, later, to remember the purple moorlands that day when, from my seat on my father's lap at the front of the doctor's car, Sawbones himself at the wheel, Mummy, my sister, Dee, Wilf and small son Miky squashed together in the back, I had watched as our car wound through the miles of glowing moor, taking us back to the city.

SIAN PHILLIPS, my widow, an estimable, haughty bird and beautiful, in the younger days, before she had even agreed to become my wife, at one time had accompanied me on a trip to Linz. There to indulge my prating of and peering at matters Adolf.

Perhaps, one evening there, my behaviour towards others had not been at its best. Perhaps I had been crass and obnoxious in bars. It's possible. Perhaps I had been disappointed that no emanations of evil had flowed up to us that winter week from Hitler's once and future city, that the place had been made remarkable to me only by the revelation that in winter all the citizenry, young or old, do slide about on skis, apparently always have, and that this had shoved into my mind an image of young Adolf scooting about so over the snow, which ludicrous picture had driven me to strong drink and shouting. Who knows? Whatever, I and Linz had proved to be not a one hundred per cent success as a mix: a point emphasised on our last night there by the refusal of my fair companion to be within yards of me, preferring rather to wrap around herself an eiderdown and to sleep in the bathtub.

Early the following morning, at dawn, having been reminded by her that peace comes not to sit but to brood, my young widow and I had agreed on a truce. Hostilities ceased, cordial relations began, hot coffee was sucked, without a backward look at the scenes of Hitler's childhood, we pointed my old MG at Bavaria and the lesser German alps, and off she flew.

Pottering our way through the peaks, deeps and steeps, we

swerved our mountain way to Nuremberg of the rallies. Dotted around the slopes, Grimm, Struwwelpeter and Rapunzel, the daintily mad follies of Schlosser Ludwig and his ilk sprout up; exquisitely slender and refined from out of the points of steep, coarse, isolated mounds. Thrilling, in the bright morning, grand and comical, all fluted and fabulous the slim soaring towers with their fancy turrets made, surely, of marzipan and gingerbread.

Solid enough, though; solid as myth or fairy's tales.

At Nuremberg of the rallies, over welcome breakfast, my widow had surprised me by listening with interest to my telling of the boyhood conviction I had held that the way to stop the war immediately was to kill Hitler. It is possible that I did not mention to her that I had considered also that there had been no better man for the job than Secret Agent Merlin, occupied in Hunsbeck, smoking an illicit cigarette in the air-raid shelter, but she asked me if I had read *Rogue Male* by Geoffrey Household. I hadn't. 'You should,' she said to me, that time at Nuremberg; her voice, I fancy, and manner freshened by a sleep in the bath. 'It might do you a lot of good.'

When first she read it, she had considered it to be a spiffing, beautifully written romantic thriller. On going to university she had found *Rogue Male* to be a cult book among students.

Geoffrey Household had been a brave and intelligent soldier and an official but heterodox servant of his country. From 1934 on, having first heard Hitler on the wireless and then having scrutinised his man thoroughly as he was able, Household had lobbied the military and political powerful with his strongly argued suggestion that practical plans be made to assassinate Hitler. If plans had been made they had not been executed and, in 1939, *Rogue Male* was published. The book describes the predicament of a man determined to assassinate a vicious dictator, head of the totalitarian government of a European country, and at once avert a possible war in Europe while avenging the slaughter of his Jewish lady love. The attempted shooting takes place up a little alp, not wholly dissimilar in description from the Obersalzburg, near Berchtesgaden, where Hitler had a hut.

The hunter is alone: feigning a rough-shoot, he has bivouacked, walked, climbed and crawled his way up the woodland slopes, is in telescopic sight of his quarry, when the gentlemen in peaked caps and black jodhpurs drop on his head and, later, sharpen their rubber truncheons on his testicles, and even as his fingernails are being pulled out with pincers, the black-clad policemen will not believe his saying that he alone and unaided was responsible for the botched assassination attempt. It had been a private individual undertaking, not made on behalf of any organisation or government of a foreign country, simply his own good idea which had gone fearfully wrong and one for which he, and only he, was solely responsible.

Geoffrey Household, now gone, did in his life often clothe his poet self in armour of pipesmoke, bluff countryman's manner and tweed, emerging occasionally crisply to pronounce on the heroes of a couple of his books, that he had simply put a chap made of the right stuff into a tight spot and had then described the events which happened as the chap strove to get himself out of it. Our rogue male does indeed escape from his uncomfortable situation and, leaving his fingernails behind, lurches off into the hills, woods and rivers, quarry to an army of pursuers, the hunter hunted, and flings himself against all hazard, determined to reach England where he will muster resources for another crack at his enemy.

Household tells his story in matchless prose; his plotting superb and unexpected, his situations, thoughts, descriptions and characters alive and leaping off the page.

At one point, having successfully reached England, our man finds himself again being hunted down. This time, however, the agents of the dictator are from much closer to home and our man, unwilling to compromise anyone else in what he looks on as his own solitary mission, does actually go to ground. He hides in an underground sett of the sort made by badgers or moles, dug by himself and to a human scale. Down a tunnel and in a hole, the killers who have tracked you down sitting on the exit and the entrance, is as tight a spot as one could wish on a chap of the right stuff.

Cunning, ingenious and lethal, the rogue male prevails over his immediate adversaries and by the end of the book, with European countries on the brink of a war caused by the dictator he has failed to assassinate, our hero finds his deadly obsession absorbed into the rightful wrath of his nation which is about to join battle with that same man and with the regime and country he both represents and governs.

Rogue male keeps his purpose still: there has been a transformation of his solitary, unswerving and private intent to avenge an evil done by destroying the doer, that is all. That others now share his known intentions merely causes him to muse on the nature of politics and government, the vigilance that one must keep against the capacity of authoritarian institutions to trespass upon traditional and cherished freedoms, and, in the predictable future, the likelihood of organised battles between authorities and outlaws becoming a commonplace in the streets of European cities.

The book *Rogue Male*, on sale in 1939, in 1948 was the subject of much mouth music over the mince in cafeterias and canteens of universities and colleges dotted around the kingdom.

The accuracy of Geoffrey Household's prophecy, his prefiguration of Hitler, his kind and his works, the very real wish that an assassin had got Hitler in 1938, coupled with the solid notion that had an assassin killed Hitler in 1938, or even that if Hitler had quit at that time, when he was considerably ahead of the game, Germany, and we with it, would probably now be hailing Hitler as the mightiest German since Frederick the Great; perhaps higher still and higher, Adolf the Greater, Redeemer of the Aryan Race, Civilisation's last Bulwark against Bolshevism, Lord of Linz in whom all knowledge, beauty and power had dwelt.

Much matter there for students, and others, to chew on. Plus the expression in thought and action, by rogue male, of Geoffrey

Household's contentious notion that there exists between all us mortals an X quality. A mutual recognition between one and another of shared and essential qualities; an intuitive sense of our sympathy with another that transcends four ale or saloon bars, patricians or plebeians, hard bed or soft bed, officers and men, gentlemen v. players, masculine, feminine, prince, pauper, Arthur, Martha, skin or tongue. An instinctive perception that, for a while, and in a particular circumstance, the one can depend on the other.

Often it is less a wish that the other X quality man or woman would do something, more a hope that she or he would not.

> O, what is he doing
> The great god Pan
> Down in the reeds by the river?

Piping hot in the tune that Geoffrey Household sang, I fancy, when Geoffrey wrote *Rogue Male*.

TIMES BY; one day in Ireland, at Inchgoole, solitary, glum, the dog having died, other cases altering, the rain flogging down, humiliated at snooker on my own table, dispossessed of pennies at poker in the police station, the tummy aching, the peninsula sodden, the old sea troubled, the little horses stabled, the fire gone out, a window gone in and the times that were in it cheerless and dim. An old poem, I fancy, in my mind to keep me company, an old Irish poem in an English version:

> In a wintering island by Constantine's halls,
> A bittern calls from a wineless place,
> And tells me that hither he cannot come
> Till the summer is here and the sunny days.

When he crosses the stream there and wings o'er the sea,
A fear comes to me he may fail in his flight –
Well, the milk and the ale are drunk every drop,
And a dram won't stop our thirst this night.

That was about the size of it, that day when the telephone rang in my high, stone house, hidden from the roads, myself alone in it. It was Solly at London, calling me from the BBC.

Had I heard of a book called *Rogue Male*? There was a script of it written by Frederic Raphael. A film of it for television. To be directed by Clive Donner. Would I be interested in playing the male of the title? Should he send me the script?

At some point in my professional life there had come to me an inexplicable sense that, when a script has been sent to me, I can tell if it is going to be any good or not from a look at its envelope. The script that Solly had promised to send to me arrived post-haste at Inchgoole, and its envelope didn't look too bad at all.

Months later, a springtime day deep in rural, storybook Dorset found Clive Donner, Solly, my old mate Bletchley, Benny the Mole, Geoffrey Household and me loitering on the grass below the unlevelled mound of a bustling cornfield there, and chuntering easily of matters various. Beside and below us we could see the ford of a stream, a high-hedged lane to it curving away into trees, hills and the buttocky tillage and grazing fields of this most pastoral of English counties. Heartland of Thomas Hardy, here; home and enchantment to T. S. Eliot; miles away only from where T. E. Lawrence had lived and died; a few fields from where, gouged into the white chalk under the green of the high hill rising steeply above his village, the enormous giant of Cerne Abbas stands, his great, jovial prick as stiff and splendid now as it had been before the arrival of the Romans, and at whose huge feet stands a house which, one time, I rented awhile and lived in for a happy summer.

The contents of the envelope had proved as promising as its

cover, and now we were a few days only away from finishing our filming of *Rogue Male*, work which from beginning to end had been for all of us, it seemed, an engrossing, satisfying task, and one which had given me a sensation of somehow resolving a chord which had hummed in my mind since boyhood.

Clive, a valued friend and an excellent director, trust and respect for each other forged professionally and successfully a decade and more ago, told Geoffrey of how he had invited me over to London before filming began to assist him in choosing the cast. How the first name that he had mentioned, a glance at a photograph by me, and one telephone call had secured for us our beautiful, doomed Jewish heroine. We both told Geoffrey of how, when the word was on the street that we were going to make the film, members of my profession had been tumbling down the telephone, out of letters, springing through doors and insisting that they be cast in *Rogue Male*.

Bletchley, chum, colleague, my partner in many a bump and prank, playing the murderous English toff, muttered diffidently that he was sure there were many other actors who could play the part just as well as he, but that when he had read the script he had been quite unable to think of one.

We talked of how, when we had realised how real and earnest was the interest being shown in us, Clive and I had deliberately trailed our coats at a cocktail party where we had reckoned half the population of London's small cinema world was likely to be. How our feet had not been even near the trough before we had been collared by an eminent author wanting to know if it was true that we were about to make a film of *Rogue Male* and, that if it was, then who was going to play the solicitor? How, throughout the making of the film, it had been unlikely for me to play scenes involving, say, a ticket office, a farm or a tailor's shop, without meeting again actors I admired and had worked with in my earlier days in the profession, clipping a ticket, leaning on a pitchfork or measuring an inside leg.

Unforgettably, of course, Alistair Sim, dying as comfortably as possible in his bed, cared for by nurses and doctors, and, much more important to Ali, by loving goodwife Naomi who had told him what I was up to. 'Peter will need me to play his uncle, Naomi, where and when will we be filming? Naomi, Naomi, why is it that after half a century of close association I still find myself having to repeat things to you? Think and be reasonable, Naomi: no one but I can play Peter's uncle properly; I am willing and, if the film-makers get a wriggle on, able to play him; it follows that I shall play the part of Peter's uncle.'

And he did. He mustered for us one last display of his rare and sensitive genius, wrapped in a towel, arrogant and hilarious, affectionate, indomitable, he played his final scene with me wreathed in the steam of a Turkish bath in Jermyn Street. Shortly after we had finished the film, Alistair died.

Benny the Mole, ditch-digger, dyke-builder, earth-worker of all sorts, happily showed us how he had made the burrow and the chamber in which rogue male goes to ground. Although he had been inspired in his design by the example of fox, mole, badger, the finished subterranean accommodation was very much his own invention and we would be lucky to find its like in any other parish that we might care to look at, here or anywhere else. Certainly I spent many days down in it and can say now that no set, before or since in theatre or films, had felt more apt in form and function or had been more simply comfortable, than Benny the Mole's set, dug down deeply into the ground, those days in Dorset.

Solly told of what we had named 'swastika' day. It not being 1938, time and events had made unnecessary the nice rectitude that Geoffrey Household had shown towards his dictator. Geoffrey had refrained from naming him. We had had no similar and sensible restraint or inhibition and we had called Hitler Hitler.

Came the day that we were to film the actors playing Hitler and his more recognisable satraps, Goering, Goebbels, Heydrich, Himmler, as seen from rogue male's distant point of view, or in close-up through the telescopic sight on his rifle, and I had a welcome day off.

When making a film, the days on which one can lazily eat breakfast, read a newspaper, uncrumple oneself from deep sleep and so be fed, informed and smoothed to meet whatever doings may present themselves, come rarely enough and this contrast with the other days of swigged coffee, slit-eyed blunderings at washing, shaving and finding one's trousers, all before the sparrows phart, is surely to be savoured. Solly had arranged that his executive duties for the day would include not having breakfast on foot, would indeed provide him with time to enjoy a sit-down number with me, to be followed by the pair of us motoring a few miles to indulge ourselves in a film-maker's holiday: as spectators at the scene which our crew would be filming of the Führer and his bunch of loathsome nasties gaily romping about on the terrace of Hitler's house. The Wye Valley was behaving very well as Bavaria and a fine house, built high, overlooking landscaped gardens and farther woodlands, had been cast as the Berghof, Hitler's happy home on the Obersalzburg.

We arrived to find the chosen house draped in the red, white and black of Nazi bunting, the crooked cross of the swastika limp with menace in the still morning air, clothing what had been a pleasant home in the bold and twisted colours and emblem of the Third Reich.

The pair of us to make-up and wardrobe trailers next, to see what effect the addition of uniforms, peaked caps, armbands, dog-whips, jackboots, moustaches, wigs, scars, spectacles and greasepaint had had on our friends the actors playing their roles as the Aryan master-race élite. Goering was having yet more sponge rubber stuffed into the heaving tummy of his fancy tunic, Goebbels and Himmler were discussing the likelihood of Vivian Richards, the West Indies batsman, posting the red leather ball to all parts of parks throughout the cricketing world for the next two decades and Hitler was quietly chewing a sausage sandwich. There was sport to be had as the Nazi élite eventually wandered on to the balcony set; admiration at the verisimilitude achieved by the make-up, the wardrobe and the actors mingling not at all incongruously with ripe raspberries and shouted *heils* seasoning the normal morning greetings of the film crew and the cast, and the pretty sight of a clutch of stormtroopers, SS and Gestapo men outdoing each other in a jackbooted heel-clicking contest.

Grey the day had been, though; with an occasional squirt of drizzle and a sly breeze creeping in from time to time to stir the drooping swastika into sudden and obscene life. Solly my friend, the Irish Jew, was here and there, solving this problem, settling that difficulty, calling on the field telephone to arrange those matters, dressed against the wet nip in a long raincoat and a Homburg hat, borrowed for the purpose from the wardrobe.

For perhaps two hours I stayed there, watching as Clive directed a scene, chatting to a prop or a sound man, looking at the film lights as the sparks wheeled them around, noting how accurately the actor had adopted Hitler's stance and stride, amused by the soldiery, stubbing out their fag ends and springing to Teutonic attention when the camera rolled, but all the while my eyes were being drawn to that hateful swastika flag and eventually I found myself altogether out of sorts, fed to the teeth, unhappy and sick to the guts. It had seemed wiser for me to quit the scene, to shift down to my caravan parked below on the road, to get warm, to find a car and get out of there, to go back to the hotel, to brood, to read a book, to get drunk, to fall in love with a passing waitress, any bloody thing except stay there, but where was Solly?

No Solly.

Down to the caravan, odd, the door's unlocked, never mind, all a thief would get would be a little practice, into the vehicle, close the door, light a cigarette, puff it, feel a little better.

A voice from the bunk bed. 'Am I in your way?' It's Solly. Solly sitting on the bed, the raincoat buttoned to his chin, its collar turned up to his ears, the Homburg hat pulled down over his eyes.

'Not at all, Solly. You all right?'

'Am I fuck.'

'What's up?'

'The souls poncing about pretending to be Nazis don't bother me. It's that swastika. It makes me feel very Jewish.'

'It makes me feel murderous.'

'Precisely.'

'Shall we piss off?'

'Let's.'

As we drove off, our way took us past a sight of the beflagged house. My eyes, of course, were drawn for an instant to the flag and its crooked cross. Solly's eyes, too, but he looked at it more deliberately than I; looked at it through the window until the moving car took it from his sight and left the damned thing flapping behind us as we drove away from it. Wordless we had sat in the back of the motor, Solly withdrawn into the raincoat, under the hat, and I could sense my mild, clever, educated friend riven by an ancient indignation.

Geoffrey Household had listened to our yarns that day in the sunlit Dorset field where nearby Benny the Mole's splendid burrow was dug, and, later, as Bletchley and I were setting off to drive the few miles to our digs in a wonderfully creaky old village pub, had accepted our offer of a lift. As we were gently bowling along a dipping, leafy Dorset byway, Geoffrey, who had a keen knowledge of the locality, quietly suggested that we make a small detour. This we had done and, again at Geoffrey's calmly authoritative prompting, had stopped the car opposite where a five-bar gate stood open at the entrance to a quiet, grassy, tree-lined little lane.

Without leaving the car, Geoffrey had gazed for a while at the peaceful, rustic, almost concealed and modest little track before saying, 'Up there in 1938, is where I wrote *Rogue Male*. It practically wrote itself, but when I got stuck, I would hear Hitler's voice and picture that wretched swastika, then we would be off again.'

I shall be forever grateful to my widow for introducing me to

that book and to Solly for telephoning me his news at that moment
when the day was drear and the times were hard in Ireland.

———

BUT SECRET AGENT O'Toole, codenamed Merlin, wounded in the
leg, out of Starsbottom, heading for the smoking city, the purpled
moors behind him, 1942 approaching, had had no notion that such
beautiful things were, in time, to come his way. A considerable
portion of his lively mind had been occupied in pondering
the vexsome possibility that, quite shortly, those bleak-looking
institutions known as schools might soon be opening their tightly
shut doors again and, lo, came his tenth year and that is precisely
what happened.

Through all the ginnels, alleys, roads, streets, terraces, crescents,
lanes and ways of Hunsbeck, I fancy, roamed out legions of school
inspectors. Officious, important and pitiless men armed with
nets, lassos and branding irons, rounding up throngs of fleet,
wilful, raggedy-arsed and free-ranging, snotty-nosed, lusty boys
and having cornered us, roped us, netted us, marked, named,
known and numbered us, had herded us struggling and yelping,
trussed and tied, into those gloomy piles of bricks and mortar,
chalk, blackboard, whacking canes and inkwells, those two years
and more uninhabited, dismal buildings called schools.

It is true that some of us had never been collared. True it is
that some of us, having been collared, wrenched ourselves loose
from this violent bondage, once more to bullock freely through
railway-line ravines, gasworks and flaxmill canyons and the cool,
peaceful meadowlands on the roof of Pints' warehouse.

Hooky had been turned in by his grandpa. After a lifetime
bearing the burdens of a heavy labouring man, Grandpa had
interested himself in the reading books which Hooky had been
given to study in his peacetime days of attendance at an infants'
school and Grandpa, having grabbed the gist of this business of

literacy, had taught himself to read by daily bending his rough old head over the poems of William Cowper.

Hooky had gone quietly.

Me too, comparatively, having been snared by a brawny chap wearing a bowler and bearing a brolly; I had submitted to being led into a church hall where a hugely stout woman wearing a fat face the colour of corned beef had loudly enticed from me my name, age, address, parentage, previous record, had banged down these particulars on to their appropriate form, hammered down a rubber stamp, shivered her trestle table with the effort of writing on a pink piece of paper the name and location of the school that she had deemed appropriate, had hugely thrust the slip of paper at me with fat-fingered hands and had then turned her vast attention on to the next young bronco standing there, picking his nose and thinking nostalgically of the former days of blackouts bombs and freedom.

Boilerby Street. Monday. 8.45 a.m. sharp. This is ridiculous. Not only is the Truetodeedle Song unheard of and unsung in this quite horrid establishment, but also the Our Father, with or without its proper words, is left unchanted.

Nor are other prayers of any sort said here. We say no grace to thank our God before or after meals; indeed there are no meals. Nothing is served here before or after which one could possibly be grateful. What can one say to a spoonful of halibut liver oil? When a tiny tin of concentrated orange juice has sickeningly gone down one's throat, immediately to reappear but from down one's nose, can one in truth pray God to bless the whole arrangement? Not a hymn is sung, not a church visited, there is no picture of baby Jesus and his blessed Mum, let alone a crucified Christ, hanging on these walls. Nobody goes to confession or benediction or even to Mass.

The buzz in the urinal is that for the duration of the war the school will be non-denominational, which is a fancy way of saying that every heathen child in Hunsbeck has been transported here.

Yes, and one half of the penitentiary has been given over to girls. You should cock an ear to their chirruping, that will thicken it for you.

Other than my name which, when stated, had given the big geezer in the double-breasted suit, the meaty headmaster, cause to groan, the only question put to me, from the same heavy source, had been whether I was church or chapel. Well, what should one have answered to such a curious enquiry other than that I go to both? And to abbeys, cathedrals, convents, priories, minsters, indeed to any consecrated premises so long as it own a denomination and that that be Catholic. That had gone down a treat with Double-breasted Heavy Meat.

He had fair erupted from behind his desk, had made a great gargling rush at me, shaken me as though I were a bedsheet, landed a round-arm, meaty thump to the back of my nut, had scooped me up from the dog-shelf, ignored all my protests and suggestions, twisted up both my arms behind my back, had frogmarched me along corridors, had flung open a door, pitched me into a stuffed, silent classroom and in it now sit I, while all around me squat dozens of pagan boys, tight-mouthed, shuffling, intimidated little heathens, each behind his cramped, lidded, little wooden desk, and staring in expectant perplexity at the withered, club-footed, surgical-booted, crooked frame of Miss Vixer, a peevish, nasty and a malevolent old bitch.

This is absurd, Miss Vixer, absurd; why would you assume that I, just one among these many godless children sitting here at your twisted and your stunted foot, should know anything at all about this long division? Why, the scrape alone of your chalk on board would make a cobble wince, your voice is a harsh crude blister on my ears that like well melody. These words of yours so sharply croaked of numbers which won't go into other numbers, necessitating that the next number be brought down and four nines are thirty-six, you bark, and so put down the six and carry the three. Where should I carry this three? There? Why? Four ones arc four and three is seven, you yelp, yes, I see that all right, as I see that nineteen into eighteen won't go, but why should it want to? Put a nought and bring down the next number? Why? Oh, they are all places are they? A nought there and the logical thing will be to have a nine or perhaps an eight? Put one and carry the eight, multiply, subtract and have remainders, you rasp, and always show my working neatly in the rough column at the side of the sum.

Now, nineteen into a hundred and seven will go and my multiplication tables will show if a figure is too high or too low, you shriek. So seven nines are sixty-three are they? Put down three and carry the six, either into the working column or the rough sum. Right. What's this? Fifteen into seventy-nine goes five times making seventy-five, put the five above the nine and the seventy-five below the seventy-nine, take away seventy-five from seventy-nine to find the remainder and if it took a man a week to walk a fortnight, how long would it take Miss Vixer to pull out a splinter from her arse wearing boxing gloves?

These long divisions and these problems, madam, are quite without my mental grasp, as are those cyphers, those symbols chalked up on the blackboard which squeaks still from all your scraping on it.

You did not know it, you venomous old bag, but you had before you one formed not unlike Eliot, G.'s Tom Tulliver, 'a boy born with a deficient power of apprehending signs and abstractions'. By shrieking at me, by pulling my hair, my ears, by cutting down hard on the back of my hands the edge of your ruler, you tried forcefully to elicit from me knowledge of non-existent facts because, Miss Vixer, you had a fixed opinion that the facts were existent. You thought that because I was stupid at signs and abstractions I must be stupid at everything else.

Not so, madam bag, not so, for I understand that ye shall know them by their fruits. Do men gather grapes of thorns? Figs of thistles? Every good tree bringeth forth good fruit, but a corrupt tree bringeth forth evil fruit. A good tree can't bring forth evil fruit, nor a corrupt tree good fruit. That makes sense.

When a horse wins a race, for every length it wins by, it can be handicapped in its next race by carrying in its saddle three pounds of lead for each winning length. A length is the length of the horse. Win by three lengths, horse, and in your next race you may carry nine pounds of lead. At three pounds a length, three times three pounds means carrying nine pounds of lead. That makes sense.

In a cricket match, if it's been agreed that there will be twenty overs after six thirty, and the side batting needs one hundred and twenty runs to win, that means they have to score six runs an over. Six balls in an over means getting a single run off every ball bowled. Not easy but quite possible and that makes sense.

Mutinous, my heart, I sit in the playground, knocking back my milk, for which gift of thy bounty I do thank God, gnawing on the sangwidges my mother made me for to take to this penal colony, knowing well that if Clubfoot or Double-breasted Meat as much as bawl, leave alone strike at me, then all will split.

Handbell rings, back to classroom clump the boys, obedient, cowed, jumpy most of us, a bit shirty some, defiant others, all, however, squeeze into our depressing, comfortless desk seats, attending on the voice of Vixer as it gouges into our souls.

'If it takes six men six and a half hours to dig six holes six and a half feet deep, how long will it take one man to dig a hole three and a quarter feet deep? O'Toole?'

'Three and a quarter hours, Miss.'

'Right. Well, if O'Foole can get one right I must make the next problem more difficult.'

You wrong me shamefully, you vicious woman, when you twist my name into a mockery. It is my name, and my father's name, and his father's name and the name of their fathers' fathers. Our name reaches back for unknown generations and out of Ireland have we come, great hatred, little room, to live and love and work and fight as free men not as bonded savages, so here is my inkwell

Peter O' Toole. At sea.
Baltic. 1951.

in your kisser; drink it down and rave and splutter; give me a hold of that ruler; shall I beat and beat and beat you? Come not near me now, old bullywoman, for I will surely kick your crooked limb and stamp upon your malformed hoof. Away you go, you inky crone; go weep, go hobble, go sob, go limp away to shout for Meat and Double-breast.

Now, who's with me? Now who will stand at my right hand and quit this brig with me? Not one of you? Right. Then I will split this scene immediately, not as I would wish, ringed with bold companions, but in far better company: alone.

It is said that true courage will do without witnesses what others may do in front of all the world; my puny rebellion fell far short of that keen assessment; it fell, along with my inflamed indignation, slowly down into my rapidly striding, polished black shoes when I realised, as I marched from the school and headed for home, that I was still bearing Miss Vixer's ruler in my fist.

My rash and gunpowder glow drifted from me entirely when I entered the house and found it empty. The hush of the house crept quietly into me and so I put the ruler on the arm of Daddy's chair before swiftly scarpering away down to the ginnel over the railway, there to mingle with other truant boys, from whose heedless swagger I could inhale determination and strength.

No. Damn their eyes. No one will ever again be let abuse me and insult me so without a certain reckoning. No. Come what may, I do not care, I am that I am. Bollocks!

> Don't Care was made to care,
> Don't Care was hung,
> Don't Care was put in a pot
> And stewed till he was done.

Not exactly, but there had been a bit of a fuss all right.

Bowler Hat, a Very Important Raincoat and even Double-breasted Head Meat itself turned up to rat tat tat on our front door but they were all greeted by Flora MacDonald Hoots MacFerguson, my mother, who gave to each a fluent and articulate savaging, bade them all good day, shut the door, and had then firmly ordered me to remove the stupid grin from my face.

Later she made a telephone call.

Himself came strolling down the street that fine weekend. Fag in his gob, hat on his head, long legs lazily dancing him along, goodies in his pockets, happiness and hugs for us and, in his singular way, he gave his full and grave attention to the matter being bruited about while maintaining an air, detached, amused, which brought a clear calm tension into what previously had been only a sort of flurry.

Came Monday morning, his billycock on and his Crombie around him, he slotted the ruler up the left sleeve of his jacket and sauntered out to pay a call on the headmaster at Boilerby Street School.

What he had said, or done, or agreed on, disputed over or whatever had gone on at the school that morning I will never know but he had come back looking very much the same as he had done when he went, bar his having safely returned the ruler.

'That Miss Vixer is tasty,' he commented. 'The governor's only a tub of lard. That should be the end of that little donkey derby.'

He was right. Official permission was granted for me to find a place at a Catholic school in the area, not a word was said about any petty incident, and there the matter closed.

Later, I learned why he had shoved the ruler up his left sleeve. During the race-track wars and the protection racket extortions of the 1920s in London and the courses of southern England, up his sleeve is where he had kept Kennedy. 'Kennedy' had been my father's name for a poker, a whimsy based on the Brown and Kennedy murder of a policeman. After being shot and killed, the eyes of the constable had remained open. Kennedy, it seems, had been convinced that his reflection was in the policeman's eyes and would remain fixed there. Kennedy had not wanted any likenesses of himself lying around and so he had heated up a white hot poker and had effaced his supposed image by poking it out of the dead man's eyes.

Brown and Kennedy had been caught and hanged but Kennedy lived on up my old Pop's sleeve in the shape of a protecting poker. The ruler had gone back to the school in the position formally occupied by Kennedy, but, one assumes, only as in a form of handy transportation. None of your tempered Toledo blades for Daddy, nor yet a shooter, nor a coke-hammer: a poker called Kennedy.

———

You would surely have enjoyed the next school: I did, for the less than an hour that I was there.

Some bright shiners had stuffed paraffin-soaked wadding into a school desk, had sealed the desk with yards of that ubiquitous, brown, wartime sticky paper, had somehow ignited the wadding and the entire issue had combusted, smoked hellishly and merrily, before exploding into a fire bomb at the back of a classroom in a Catholic school at Hunsbeck.

Fire engines had arrived, and ambulances, ARP men, the Home Guard, policemen, soldiers, the school had been evacuated and Daddy and I had occupied this lacuna in the scheme of organised education with a game of soccer; a ginnel for our pitch, an empty condensed milk tin for our ball, and when the match was over and we had lost or drawn or won, thus, I fancy, spake Captain Pat on the war: 'What price Hirohito, Tojo and the Rising Sun team making matchsticks of the American fleet at Pearl Harbor? That can't have been on many people's cards. The papers called it a cowardly act of aggression and yet I don't know; if you intend to kick a man to death there's no point sending him a postcard. The balloon has gone up all over the bloody world, son, way up, and my money says it will stay up and not be in a hurry to come down again.

'Ye bugs, didn't we throw the towel in at Singapore without

laying a glove on the Nips? Now the Nips are rushing about all over Asia sticking bayonets into anything that moves.

'Still and all, the Yanks have joined in the frolic now and the odds against us must have shortened slightly, shorter than they'd been eighteen months back, for if the Germans had invaded us and if we had taken up Churchill's suggestion to fight them on the beaches and on the landing places, it would have boiled down to German paratroopers, stormtroopers and armoured divisions being taken on by the squire firing nuts, bolts and rusty nails from his fowling piece, a scoutmaster with a carving knife tied to the handle of a broomstick and me heaving half bricks at their heads.

'But it didn't happen, thanks be to Jesus, and now the Huns and the Comrades have had a snowball fight in Russia which has ended in a draw. They tell me the winter times are a bit nippy near Moscow so if Hitler is going to knock over Russia, he'll need to do it this summer or it's a hundred to plenty he'll find himself starting off Napoleon's mark. Now, you toddle back to Mummy, tell her the school has been blown up, I'm off to see a man about a dog.'

———————

MY FATHER and mother had lobbied authorities both secular and divine and it had been agreed that I be let travel daily from south of the city to the north and attend again the school that I had gone to as an infant. These arrangements had taken a while and during that while I had been scooped up and dumped into a Franciscan establishment which stood, pertinently I suppose, in the middle of an area wholly composed of mercantile mills. Mills of all sorts, grinding and turning and threshing around this latest instalment into the great sum of my education. One aesthete and joker had had his mill built up to the scale, form and pattern of an ancient Egyptian temple of the dead.

'Right, lads, I want nothing dark and satanic for my workers, let's have something dark and Isisic, either road the buggers who will sweat in it are dead meat.'

My stay there had been short, my relief at being once more among Christians immeasurable, and all of us, harum-scarum boys, outnumbered nuns, hellfire-eating priests and even, it had seemed, the very bricks of the building had joined brave and lusty amidst the saw, tread and loom of the mills, in chorus after rapturous chorus of the Truetodeedle Song.

> Faith of our fathers, Holy Faith,
> We shall be true to thee till death.

My way to and from Brother Moon's learning mill had led me to a stretch of railway line which curved out of a tunnel, straightened immediately after it passed under a small bridge, and then ran on and away to points west of the place. This was undiscovered country to me and I had been delighted to see that from the embankment above the tracks onc could watch the trains as they splendidly chugged and puffed from out of the tunnel, steamed and clanked around the curve and having passed under the bridge, they picked up speed and went whistling and clattering away.

One afternoon I spotted a small knot of ruffian boys standing on the edge of the embankment near the bridge and staring at the tunnel's maw. The moment a train lumbered steaming out of the tunnel, one lad split away from the others, scrambled down a wall lining the tracks, carefully placed something on the line, jumped away, pressed his back to the wall and an instant later the train careered past him, feet only away from his face. When the last carriage had passed him, the boy began searching around the spot on the line where he had placed his mysterious something.

A whoop of joy signalled that the lad had found whatever it was he had been looking for and by the time I had joined his group of mates, the boy had clambered back up the wall, was standing in a scrum of chums, his arm stretched out proudly and in the upturned palm of his hand sat a hot, thin, shining, round metal wafer, the desired fruit, as I was soon to learn, of placing a halfpenny coin on a railway line and having a steam engine roll over and flatten it for you. The strict rules of this sport demanded that the bearer of the halfpenny be not allowed to begin his descent to the line until the train appeared from out of its tunnel, the distance from the tunnel to the bridge being roughly fifty yards, the time that it took the iron chuff-chuff to roll along that yardage constituted the maximum period permitted for the bearer to tumble down the wall, plonk the ha'penny on the track, jump back flat against the siding and close his eyes as the locomotive crushes steadily before him, spitting out sparks and cinders.

To attach oneself to this group of adventurers but not to dare undertake their task of having one's coin so rendered in the manner prescribed by the siding laws of copper-squashing, would have meant bowing to their collective judgement that one was 'windy', fit only to play skipping rope with tarts and so, of course, by nightfall, from head to foot filthy, knees hands fingers all grazed, heart hammering, eardrums pounding, I, no happier boy in Hunsbeck, romped my way home with my hand wrapped around a halfpenny, shiny, hot, flat, round and as squashed as one could wish.

The following afternoon and we all went copper-squashing again. This time, though, as the train came cheerfully crunching along, we had to place a pin on the halfpenny as well. By the end of the week, I had become the owner of a rare and golden disc, embossed all with a cruciform of silver. It was the exhibition to my new classmates of this fine and shining object that had directly led to my first fight. Scuffles, plenty; elbow digs, scores; slaps, kicks, tugs, begot or bestowed, countless; tangled heaps of fury, more than enough, but, a fight, a single-combat, bare-knuckled fight at an agreed time and place and with spectators, never.

A boy in my class, my own age but a bit taller, had grabbed my hard-wrought medallion, examined it carefully, had clearly been impressed but was now reluctant to hand it back. My request that he return to me my property had been countered by his suggesting that I make him, which suggestion had been punctuated by his fetching me a sharp dig to that part of the upper arm much favoured by little boys flinging fists: the side just below the shoulder, made mostly of gristle and bone, which when accurately struck immediately sends out hot shocks of aching gyp.

A flying jump on him had seemed to me to be an appropriate response and, having successfully landed on him, the impetus skittled the pair of us onto the floor, knocked my treasure from his thieving grasp, propelled us into a roll and a wrestle among the desks and the booted feet of our avid fellow classmates and whose merry way had been interrupted by a call from the lookout at the classroom door telling that, even now, Sister Pudentiana Mary was flowing rapidly in our direction. While scooping up and safely pocketing my silver cross on gold, I heard urgent whispers from our classmates announcing that hostilities had only temporarily ceased, were to be continued after school and that the venue for the duel would be at the usual and approved place, a broad ginnel between two mills behind the school.

'Fight,' was the shout from the throats of boys after the liberty bell had sounded. 'Fight,' they called to boys released from other classrooms. 'Fight,' was the word as my opponent and I were bundled along among a host of lads scampering towards the preferred arena. Two sides of the square ring had been formed by brick walls of mills, the other two by ranks of roaring, flushed, rowdy boys. Jackets had been taken off, sleeves rolled up, there had been a baying and a bellowing from the others and the two of us had furiously got stuck into one another.

Be assured, my attitude before the off had been one of reluctance and dismay, but once the arms and the fists had begun flailing, the blood had banished the mind's grip and all I had known had been to fling as much knuckle or knee or elbow or foot as I could muster.

At one point a heavy bump had flung me staggering backwards

among the ringsiders, they in their turn had heaved me back into the barney, catapulted thus, a whirling piece of me had solidly landed flush on the nose of the other fighter, down he had gone, heavily down, and to my great relief he had stayed down, right down where he had been put.

The fight was finished; I had won.

From the moment that school was out, to the final knock-down thump, the rapidity and tumbling propulsion of events had left me more bewildered than triumphant, and as the mob of little boys began to disperse, crowing or laughing or chattering, some to wander away up the alley, some to group about me with praises, one to hold my arm victoriously aloft, another to help me on with my coat, my relief had begun to puff up into an exhilaration, into the unperturbable confidence of a victor, when I noticed for the first time a huddle of senior boys who obviously had been taking an interest in the pugilistic antics of we small and matchstick juniors.

From their centre slouched out a loathsome looking animal, a swart, squat ape of a boy, a filthy thing in form in dress in feature, bow-legged, black and shaggy-headed, with thick, dirty arms that dangled down to end in blunt bunches of hands, a squash of a face, deep in which were stuck tiny dark stones of eyes, and his mouth was wide, open, red and slobbering.

For a frightening moment it had seemed that he had been about to give me his full attention, but after a brief and strange and brutish inspection of me, he had spat on the ground and had then lumbered over to where the loser lay. The lad that I had beaten sat sobbing on the flagstones, his head and back pressed against the brick wall, his nose bloody and with blood also on his lips, chin, hands and shirt. Next to him squatted a couple of his chums, one carrying the boy's jacket, both silent and, indeed, the ginnel had gone quiet.

I had turned away to leave, my instincts tugging me away from that place, when I had heard thick grunts of speech, rough-mouthed words telling of punches; how to punch, how not to punch, what should not be called a punch, what should be called a punch, and I had looked back. His two companions had moved away from where the bleeding boy crouched, the grunting brute was hauling up the lad by his bloody shirt and having heaved him onto his feet, he began to demonstrate with his big fists what he had meant by his hoarse words. Punch after punch after punch he rammed into the jolting face of the vanquished boy until the lad toppled face down and senseless onto the ground where, as though to end his lesson, the thug booted a vicious kick into the ribs of that unconscious boy.

It had been a confused conqueror called O'Toole who, heartsick that night, had trudged home alone.

'Around the world thoughts shall fly in the twinkling of an eye.'

A PROPHECY made in the nineteenth century by the seer and witch Old Mother Shipton, one that, I fancy, for us in England in the years of 1941 and 1942 had been perhaps richly realised when we had turned on our wireless sets:

Good evening, this is the BBC. There'll be bluebirds
over the white cliffs of Dover tomorrow. James Joyce
the Irish novelist is dead. All Jews over the age of six
must wear the Star of David. Bubble bubble bubble.
Don't forget the diver, guv'nor, don't forget the diver,
I'm going down now. Bubble bubble bubble. Last night
Hitler's deputy, Rudolf Hess, landed by parachute in
a field near Glasgow. Rissoles are to be mass produced.
Saying that it is better to die, Turkey has refused to
join the Axis. There were angels dining at the Ritz.
It is feared that the aviatrix Amy Johnson has been

drowned. All single women between twenty and thirty
are to be called up, boys and girls between sixteen and
eighteen must also register. Hitler and Mussolini have
declared war on the United States. Can't you hear me
calling, while my tears are falling? For its courage in
enduring four months of daily bombing, the island of
Malta has been awarded the George Cross. My name is
Fumf the spy, I go, I come back. In the sands of North
Africa the Eighth Army has been given a new name:
the Desert Rats. Time is something which is measured
by a clock, would you agree, Professor Joad? It depends
what you mean by time. Reinhard Heydrich, the butcher
of Moravia, has been assassinated outside Prague.
Colonel Chinstrap, will you kindly desist? I don't mind
if I do. In conditions of the utmost secrecy, the Prime
Minister, Mr Winston Churchill, and the President of
the United States, Franklin D. Roosevelt, have met at
sea and have proclaimed in their Atlantic Charter that
the aggressor nations must be disarmed and that after
the war all men shall be enabled to live in freedom from
fear and want. Our romance was different from the
rest, we met one rainy afternoon. Under the command
of Frank 'Bomber' Harris the RAF have struck back
at the Axis, raining thousands of tons of bombs down
on Lübeck, Essen, Cologne, Naples, Tripoli. Jelly Roll
Morton the jazz man is dead. I need women power for
the war effort, I cannot offer them a delightful life but I
want one hundred thousand women to step forward and
suffer some inconvenience with a determination to see us
through. Can I do you now, sir? Not now, Mrs Mopp.
Right, sir, it's being so cheerful that keeps you going.
In reprisal for the killing of Heydrich, all the men and
boys of the Czechoslovakian village of Lidice have been
shot. In conditions of the utmost secrecy, Churchill and

Stalin have met in Moscow to proclaim their intention
of the complete destruction of Hitlerism. There'll be joy
and laughter and peace ever after tomorrow. The King's
brother, the Duke of Kent, has been killed. Because of his
gallantry and brilliance in the North Africa Campaign,
the Desert Rats have made an unlikely hero of the
German general Rommel, nicknaming him the Desert
Fox. Virginia Woolf the writer is dead. Her parasol went
gay and I was in the way, she didn't even say I'm sorry.
After last night's blanket bombing of German cities, Air
Marshal Frank Harris has freely admitted that there
were no specific targets, he says he intends to disrupt the
German economy and destroy the morale of the civilian
population. Admitting heavy losses, the British have
evacuated the island of Crete. It's the boogie-woogie
bugle boy from company B. The United States has
declared war on Japan and its Axis partners. We're
going to hang out the washing on the Siegfried Line. The
name of the Norwegian premier, Quisling, will in future
be synonymous with treachery and collaboration with
an enemy. America is not training three million men
to play tiddlywinks with the Germans. Keep smiling
through just like you used to do. It is estimated that
between three and four hundred thousand Jews have
been systematically murdered in Poland. HMS *Hood* has
been sunk, HMS *Ark Royal* has been sunk, the *Bismarck*
has been sunk. I shall return, said General Douglas
MacArthur as he left the Philippines for Australia. Our
romance it started on the spot without the aid of stars
or the moon. India has been promised Dominion status.
The Nazi U-boat base at St Nazaire was left a raging
inferno after British Commandos stormed ashore from the
destroyer *Campbeltown*. A look, a smile, a sigh, I still can't
figure why but that's how our romance began. In Las

Vegas the actress Carole Lombard has been found among
the twenty-two dead in the wreck of a TWA airliner. The
Allies have failed to halt the Japanese in Malaya. I may
be right and I may be wrong but I'm perfectly willing to
swear. In a lightning raid, American B25s have bombed
the Japanese capital of Tokyo. My Yiddisher mama.
Germany is pushing back the Eighth army. Russia has
repelled the Panzers. The United States have routed
the Japanese in the battle of Midway. It's a lovely day
tomorrow.

From Jutland to the Iberian peninsula, in 1942, the entire
mainland of Western Europe was under the jackboot. To the
north, Denmark and Norway were crushed and the heel of the
boot was stubbing out Finland. In central and in southern Europe,
the goosestepping jackboots had marched over the carcasses of
Czechoslovakia and Poland and stood now on the backs of
the Ukraine, Yugoslavia, Hungary, Romania, Bulgaria, Albania,
Greece; from these countries Hitler has loosed out eastward his
tanks, armoured vehicles, bombers, fighters, his men and machines
of war, to fight out with Russia the most immense land battle that
the world has ever known. From the Maghreb to the Middle East,
Libya, Algeria, Tunisia, Egypt, all are being rolled over by the
Germans and their Italian allies while we, Lord love us, have
formed an alliance with the United States of America and have
declared war on Japan. The Japanese have politely noted our
aggressive declaration and are heavily occupied in carving up
and crushing, from Manchuria to Hong Kong, half of the whole
of China, the countries of Malaya, Singapore, Korea, Vietnam,
Cambodia, Thailand, Burma, Java and the Philippines, are rapidly
advancing over all parts of South-Eastern Asia and are threatening
Australia and New Zealand.

From the China seas, the Pacific, the Mediterranean, to the
Atlantic, the North Sea, the Baltic Sea and the Black Sea, the
world is at war.

Here in Merry England, isolated, embattled, yet we shall be merry, England, we cheerfully somehow chug on. To our right, bar six north-eastern countries, the holy land of Ireland is technically neutral but, at Inchgoole, the riflemen of the Irish-speaking Connacht Brigade are mustered with their weaponry near the Tower of Yeats at Thor, Ballylee, ready to slaughter the hordes of Hitler should they put their fancy boots on the turf and the golden gorse boglands of the road to the isles stretching down over the swing bridge to the town of Ballydangle where the men do harvest seaweed and my cousin Horseface runs a boozer.

Cosmetics are scarce here at Hunsbeck, so the mill girls wishing to be pretty and the women working in the munitions factories are dabbing on their cheeks cornflour, titivating their lips with beetroot juice, and some bold cows are painting their legs all over with gravy browning, drawing a pencil line straight down from the back of their thighs, behind knees, over calves, down ankles and into shoes, thus providing a seam to the stockings they have painted on their legs.

Blessings ever be to the kindly light provided to us by the great little number eight battery, the round and dainty cardboard-wrapped small tube, the portable and sacred cell which slid into our empty flashlights and electrically supplied us with good deeds of modest beams and lit the paths of our blacked-out naughty world. When no 'alert' had been sounded, or after the welcome wail of an 'all clear', we were officially permitted to prod our careful ways aided by these demure, friendly pools of light spilling from our torches, powered all by the unassuming, for-ever blessed, number eight battery.

Precious, rare objects that they were, you may imagine one's great wonder and delight when one fine night Captain Prometheus O'Toole came stooping through the door at Peartree Lane, burdened quite by armfuls of substantial, heavy wireless batteries, which he reverently, gratefully laid down on the flagstone before the open fireplace. Muttering of mysteries concerning voltages, likelihoods, possibilities and of inside information, he descended to the cellar, re-emerging swiftly bearing a hammer and a chisel. The wrappings of the large loaf-shaped batteries were quickly jemmied off, the chisel aimed into the centre of one of the glossy, black pitchlike casings. A tight grip, a sharp blow, a chink of hammer on chisel and didn't the casing split and sunder, fall into scraps and chunks, leaving only intact what was very like a hefty bundle of dozens of number eight batteries, unadorned by official labeldom?

Daddy plucked up one of the identical darlings, wrapped her around with a stripe that he tore off the *Evening News*, shoved her into an unloaded flashlight and out flowed a small, soft glow. We turned off the lights and she beamed out a chaste spot all around the room.

We were elected, we owned a source of the linklights which aided us to banish away the sightlessness of the blackout nights and made us again able to see; the cherished and splendid number eight battery.

We hoarded most, flogged some, and sprinkled the rest to neighbours; Toms old and young, one old, you may recall, one with a splitting cough. The dwarf Harold, son of old Tom, who those days permanently wore, tightly strapped to his chin and quite fitted over his eyes, his air-raid warden's tin hat, was delighted with a further instrument of vigilance and power, given to join the webbing which he always wore over his raincoat, the buckets of sand he carted hither and yon, the buckets of water he lugged to be alongside them, and the ripeness in every coil of his unsleeping stirrup pump. Watchful Harold, ready, prepared and able to combat firestorms and the battering of bombs; for he had had his fierce hour. One night an incendiary bomb had fallen onto the lavatory of a house fifty or so yards away and in the next street. By the time Harold had arrived the bomb had begun its deadly fizz and splutter. Harold had immediately started dumping buckets of sand on it, the while yelling that the women and children among the nearby occupants should flee, but that he needed men to fetch more sand by bucket or bag or in handfuls; also, would some bugger kindly attach this here spare hose to their water tap and keep the stuff pouring. A parfit gentil air-raid warden, little Harold; with wet sand the gallant man had put out the firebomb, smothering it before it could explode.

Toothless, emaciated, taller, elder brother Raymond had listed away for a soldier.

Mr and Mrs Spunk, Ernest, the Toms, Mr and Mrs Sammy were quietly happy with their unassuming torches and one night, one merry Saturday night, our door was knocked on late, was opened and had revealed swaying Toms and Sammy. Sammy said, 'Please thank Pat, Mr Toole, very much for the batteries. Before we got our torches we were blinned. This is the first night we've been able to find our way back from the pub.'

Neighbour Spunk, who regularly rocked his knotted, twisted frame to and from his double shifts of heavy unskilled labour, had grandly squandered away a few bursts of his rare illumination by pointing his flashlight up his face and appearing at unexpected spots and moments in the dark street as a bogeyman's disembodied head, thus flinging delightful scares into me and his young son Ernest.

———————

'HOW ARE you segociating?' Podge our kinsman ganger would say, and if things were going not too badly for you, you might answer him, 'Like a daisy.'

So it was with me and my reunion with the school that I'd known as an infant. A handsome building designed in the shape of a long barn but one with high wide windows, it had been built after the Catholic Emancipation Act of 1829, opened by the Liberator himself, the Irishman Daniel O'Connell, and for me it had segociated like a daisy. An ordinary elementary school, it stood on the altogether more grand northern slopes of the city, was situated among centres of learning and medicine, had a close association with the cathedral of St Anne's, whose name it bore, and before the war had earned a reputation as being the preferred school for Catholic parents who wished their children to be prepared for entrance to the Catholic college which stood around the corner up the hill. The war had completely put the kybosh on such high-stepping notions and now the entire staff of the school was made up of the headmaster, the deputy headmaster and the senior schoolmistress, all three doing their able damnedest to shove the basics of literacy, numeracy and decency into skulls and souls, many of which had grown unaccustomed to the disciplines of learning. Raggle-taggle boys, all sorts of differing sod such as I, who drifted into the building from sundry parts of the baronry, until the classrooms fair bulged with the mass of us.

From Hunsbeck to my school and back had meant for me a daily journey of some six or so miles. A tram, a bus, and a short trot on hoof had covered the distance comfortably for me and I had relished my roamings through the jostle and bustle of a teeming wartime city. Hats, I recall. Hats. A multiplicity of tit-for-tats worn by men and women of the forces and the services. Large hats, small hats, sailor hats, bush hats, tin hats, hats with fancy tassels to them, peaked caps, round caps, floppy caps, forage caps, pillboxes, helmets, bonnets, berets, tam o'shanters, turbans, all in many and differing colours as they had bobbed along above me on the heads of their wearers.

Had I sensed, too, as my eleventh year came round to me, a lifting from our souls of dread and confusion? Had I sensed deep, deep inside us that young roots of hope and confidence had determinedly begun to grow? Half a century on, I believe that I had.

We had survived. A brave, desperate and successful rearguard stand at Dunkirk had allowed a third of a million Allied soldiers to escape to England in a superbly improvised flotilla of small ships. In the North Sea and the Atlantic the Royal Navy had prevailed over both the blockade and the U-boat war. Aided by radar and the Observer Corps the Royal Air Force had met and bested the hitherto unopposed German Luftwaffe and had won the battle of the skies over Britain. Any thoughts that Hitler may have had of invading this country had been for ever confounded. We civilians had endured and the country was no longer alone. From the Empire, the Commonwealth and the Free Forces of the occupied territories the battle was being joined, and we now had powerful allies. Not only was Uncle Joe Stalin and his Russia on our side but we had also linked arms with the noble Franklin Delano Roosevelt and his Yankee Doodle Dandies, all of us, it had seemed, resolved at last to face our attackers, and to fight and fight until our world was rid of them.

My teachers had closed their eyes at school in sorrowful tolerance of my opaque indifference to matters mathematical, had beamed out firm and generous encouragement to any aptitude that I may have shown for other subjects, and among the pupils and the priests of the cathedral and the school, friendships were being formed which endure still.

ONE CAN, when one's number eight battery has gone dud, shove it into a red hot oven, thoroughly bake or roast it, pop it back into its listless flashlight, and for a further few minutes it will cause dainty beams to utter from the torch. The nuisance is in the noisome pong which issues from the oven and floats right up one's nostrils. A fetid reek of rotten teeth and hot iron is what my young nose had discerned on receiving its first whiff. The stench which in many of our ancient European stories precedes the appearance of shapechangers. Those mysterious, magical, terrible beings who come to us in shapes of shadows and substances. As giants or whispers or wizards or as they want they will appear to us from out the pages of our books, for they can inhabit all matter.

Invisible as my Merlin when he wishes, fleshed and bloody as Loki when he wills. You may have glimpsed him in the flash of a salmon's leap. From the lofty way of an eagle he may have studied you. Earthly, now, he is the herdsman, he is the hunter, he is the infant, he is the ancient, he is the peacemaker, he is the warrior. Supernatural, he mocks us for our mortal frailties. Human, the wild unearthly women do enrapture him. Now he is insolent, wilful, capricious. Now he is wonderful, generous, mild. Now a solitary, now among multitudes, now indolent, now vigorous, now a mercy, now an abomination. Masculine and inexplicable, who see the wheel but cannot hinder the turning, these demigods and demons from our old vernacular literature; reeking of decay and molten iron.

It had been in a shape of one such wonderful and almighty creature that Adolf Hitler had appeared to the people of Germany in the later twenties of this twentieth century. The omnipotent, omniscient and omnipresent Führer, redeemer of his Aryan race.

That, one mutters, had been a prodigious change of shape for a forlorn and timid, wretched little hysteric from Linz. How had this come about? How wrought? How nourished? Cop this.

Red, red rosës. Travel with this man and you are smothered in flowers. This man is a god. In his big blue eyes like stars he is glad to see me and I am in heaven. In the morning he talks of the question of race and I am deeply moved. These are expressions of the natural creative instrument of the future determined by God. He is as a child: kind, good, merciful; as a cat: cunning, clever, agile; as a lion: roaring, great and gigantic. In the afternoon he talks of the State, of winning over the State and of the political revolution, of the creation of a New State and how we are relentlessly going to fight for it. He speaks with wit, irony, fun, sarcasm, seriousness and passion thoughts which I may well have had but have never been able to put into words. He is a prophet. 'And my head will not roll in the sand until I have fulfilled my mission', with these words he ends his prophecy. In the evening he speaks about the future architecture of the country and he is only a practical artist and architect but he fills in his pictures with his brilliant description of a new German constitution and he is a master statesman. Adolf Hitler, I love you because you are both great and simple. A genius, a born tribune, the coming dictator, a man who has everything to be a king. Farewell from him. My heart aches.

Thoughts expressed to his dear diary by that philologist from Heidelberg University the hideous Dr Josef Paul Goebbels, and in 1926. Yes, to be sure, the words had been written to be read but, still and all, the learned doctor could hardly have put such words down if the being before him had been unable at least to shape up to such descriptions, and in 1926 Adolf the Beast, Monarch of Berchtesgaden and the Bavarias, had been segociating like a daisy. In time, as Minister of Propaganda for the Third Reich, Goebbels, liberated by his master from the constraints of fact, would cynically foster and further the myth of Hitler, but at the beginning of their association in the middle twenties, there is in my view no doubt that the author and architect of that myth, the very stuff of it, had stood before him in the shape of Adolf Hitler himself.

Whatever had happened to the lank and lonely waif of Linz?

Throughout its known history our world has suffered always from a procession of tyrants and tyrannies but surely seldom if ever has there been a less likely candidate for the work than Adolf Hitler the painter from Linz.

Yes, we have been told and have read and do believe that from his earliest days he had felt himself elected to a unique and indefinable destiny. That his crude mind had been an immense engine of force, power and intelligence. That his phenomenal memory had stored and cherished a colossal store of facts and notions grasped from his reading and his experiences. That he had forgotten no hurt or slight or insult or rejection and had remembered always to meet their perpetrators with a pitiless retribution. Hatred and more hatred had animated and consoled him. Cunning, deception, delusion, cant, ruthlessness and power had been his gods, and flattery, charm, bribery, greed and hypocrisy his angels.

All too damnably well do we realise that over the long and often solitary years from his schooldays to the end of the First World War he had brooded much on the meaning and the way of all history, that to his struggling genius Providence had in simple form revealed an absolute understanding of its meaning, and that in future he both could and would dictate the way of it.

Have mercy on us but we know that his hatred of the Jews had been the poised centre of his intellectual equilibrium. That he had held modern society to be only a putrefying remnant of an ancient vigour, that in German blood alone still ran a pure inheritance to the name and vitality of humankind, and that the defeat of his Fatherland in the war had been a catastrophe for civilisation.

War, death, ruin and barbarousness had been his honour and his exultations. Why, mighty Rome itself, its legions and its Empire, had it not been undermined and subverted from inside by Jewish Christianity? Had not such great names as Attila and Alaric ridden with their glorious barbarian hordes, the Huns, Goths and Vandals, and had sacked, pillaged and destroyed utterly the cities, territories and peoples of this now enfeebled puny nation which at its mightiest had subjugated and ruled the entire known world?

He had lectured, preached and talked much on that and right well we know it, just as we had learned that by their conquest and inheritance of the lands that had formerly belonged to Rome, the leaders of the Germanic Middle Ages had certainly done no more than to obey the iron laws of history.

The grievous wretch had explained that.

We know.

Just as we know also that those iron laws had been eroded and rusted by that misnomer the Renaissance, which in fact had been a paralysing disease deliberately spread throughout Western civilisation by a plutocracy of Jews that had both infected and balked German medieval Europe from completing its historic task.

Now, he had relentlessly continued to explain, the entire continent lay stricken.

International Jewry had persuaded a decadent liberal middle class to suffocate the West under democracy and its dead weight of numbers, while in the east Bolshevism, that bastard child of Christianity fathered by the Jew Marx and fostered by the Jew Lenin, sought only the mobilisation of the masses of slaves with the object of undermining all societies.

Destiny had ordained that there yet remained hope. Endlessly had he said so.

Germany must awake! Must grasp an ember from the dying fires of culture and with force and leadership must light a brand to hand on to subsequent generations! The German people must be compelled to greatness! Must be educated to rediscover this ancient nature of ruthlessness and barbarism! Must rearm! Must understand the iron necessity of creating a new social order and with this single historical occurrence a new master race would arise!

He had made this plain over and over again. We know.

He would lead this invincible master race in the resumption of that glorious mission of blood and soil that for centuries had been neglected. He would destroy his enemies, extirpate and exterminate all alien and subhuman races and conquer again those eastward lands that by right belonged to Germany. At the centre of these territories one hundred million members of his colonising master race would form a nucleus of might as hard as steel, the Slav peoples would be pressed into serfdom, for a thousand years the swastika would fly over this magnificently barbaric German Empire, and the entire world would be rejuvenated!

Yes, we know all that. Had he not been consistently shrieking and preaching as much since 1920? What we want to know is who had let him? Who had encouraged him? For these are the ravings of a severely cracked pot indeed, one can gather earfuls of the like in every city on earth. What we want to know is why had someone not stopped that foul mouth with fair argument and hit him on the head with a coke-hammer?

What potent stuff had so thrilled through the mind, frame and tongue of the future Führer that his audiences had quailed before the dread might of his person and his arguments?

Emil Maurice who died of years in bed at Munich in 1979 at the age of eighty-two could, I fancy, have given us a hint.

You see, Alf had learned early and had learned hard the socking validity of Dr Johnson's dictum that 'Every man has the right to utter what he thinks truth, and every other man the right to knock him down for it.'

Hitler had wanted no more of that. Certainly not in the Hofbrauhaus beerhall on the evening of 24 February 1920.

Only four months in politics, already Director of Propaganda for the new born Nazis, he had twenty-five points of the party's programme to announce, an audience of two thousand to whom he would announce them, and he had insisted that during the course of his enunciation of the twenty-five points he would receive from his two thousand listeners nothing but an absolute hush. Should anyone offer so much as a single cheep of interruption they would be beaten bloody and flung out onto the cobbles.

The punters had been warned. For those who wished to attend its meetings, posters and speakers had clearly stated the Nazi party laws. Anyone not prepared to be in complete agreement with all that would be said and done had better stay away. Complete silence during all speeches. No Jews admitted. No Communists admitted. Enthusiastic applause permitted at the end of each oration. No discussion. Admission price X. Wounded soldiers half price.

To assist the audience into a perfect understanding of his laws, that February night of 1920, Hitler had formed a team of killer brutes called the Party Stouthearts. Their leader had been Emil

Maurice. Some of his men had stood facing the audience from directly under Hitler's podium, others had lined the back and the sides, all had been watchful, armed and silent.

Hitler had stood and made his points, the silences had been stretched and poignant, at appropriate moments the crowd had enthused, Maurice's men had stifled all discord, a happy Hitler had sat down again, and the triumph of his will had begun its tremendous assertion. Never again would independent and critical voices sound when he chose to speak. Never! Dissent and debate, pernicious instruments of a discredited and decaying social order, for ever would be banished from his presence. No other voice but his could truly tell his own folk what they yearned to know and think. No other voice but his could tell his own folk what they desperately wanted to hear. No other voice might sound to sully the mystical communion between his own folk and their Führer. Never! Never! Never!

The beneficial effects that this successful experiment in law enforcement and political terror had had on Hitler can scarcely be overestimated.

When untroubled by interruption or respectful disagreement, he had in the past demonstrated to a remarkable degree his powers as a randomly informed, heated and fluent, crude soliloquist. Now, unburdened from the shackles of coherent argument, confident that all doubt, dissension or alternative considerations would be bludgeoned at source, his confidence fair flowered. Five foot nine inches of Führer Hitler swelled and shimmered as his tongue tolled and soothed and seared and sounded. The miracle of the microphone made clear his voice to listeners at a distance. Electrical sound amplifiers wonderfully ringed his audiences around and wrapped them in a great chamber of his voice. Never before in mankind's history had the means to so enlarge a voice and fling it out such distances existed.

Convinced himself by all that he thought and felt, believed, imagined or envisioned, an audience became the greater part of Hitler's personality, indispensable to the wholeness of his existence. And for the first time on earth there had been great supercharged motor cars to roll the Führer and his voice along the roads, aeroplanes to fly them swiftly through the skies, telephones through which he could speak his commands to all the cities of his country and beyond, the wonder of the wireless and the radio to let his great utterances invade the privacy of houses, the quaint magic of the gramophone and its disc, records of his speeches playing round and round, over and over again, and, most awesome wonder of all: the talking picture. There, enlarged and magnified on a great screen, the brilliantly urgent focus of thousands of packed and darkened cinemas, the person and the voice of the Führer; a fabulous marvel for his amazed audiences.

So successfully had Maurice's men, the Party Stouthearts, enforced order and silence at meetings, that when Hitler became leader of the Nazis with dictatorial power, he determined to expand this house guard and to use it always as an arm of overt terror to his political will. In time, under a different commander and renamed the Sports and Gymnastic Section, the organisation became responsible for not only maintaining strict order at Nazi meetings but also for visiting disorder and violence on the meetings of other political parties. In time, armed with pistols and rubber truncheons, men from the organisation blasted through all the towns and cities of Germany. In time, equipped with weapons and men from the army, trained by professional soldiers, this dreadful presence swelled into Hitler's Stormtroopers. In time, the Stormtroopers divided into million-headed armies of brown-uniformed SA men, black-uniformed SS men and, in time, they stopped the mouths of generations.

Deep below in his bunker on 30 April 1945 the Führer had opened his mouth for the final time. Not to speak last words or to issue out incontrovertible argument but rather to admit into his mouth the inflexible fact of a gunbarrel. He had fired the gun, a bullet had smashed through brain and bone, blood had gushed and

Hitler had sprawled dead on a sofa. Himself he had shut up for ever. He had, of course, had an audience for this final eloquence. Little Eva, his mistress for fourteen years, his bride of a few hours only, had shared the sofa with her husband. Dutifully had she chewed her capsule of cyanide, had witnessed in what manly a manner Adolf could kill himself, and then she too had died, poisoned at the side of her Führer.

Minutes before his suicide, shrunken, stooped, withered and shivering, Hitler had shuffled around the ill-lit corridors at the base of the bunker, saying goodbye to his own folk. Rot from his teeth commingled with mucus had coated his lips, his words had been harsh indistinct whispers, the breath that bore them filthy.

Seconds after this suicide, deep underground and smothered in concrete, nothing had remained of the Third Reich and its creator but a hot rancid odour of gunsmoke and rotting teeth.

MERLIN HAD moved away from me awhile in 1943; he had transported my green and golden knight, Sir Yvain, away with him, but they had left me in the great company of Wilson the Wonderman from the *Wizard* comic. What with school and games and play and scrapes and books and friends and family and Wilson and all, the confusions of my early years had been clearing away rapidly and that should have been quite enough to be going on with but, do you see, the tram which had departed its stop in front of the pawnshop at 8.40 a.m. with me on it at the age of eleven had always meant my being black late for school. The 8.20 a.m. had usually rattled me on my way to assembly with minutes to spare. The 8.10, though, Lord love you, the 8.10 had bumped me into the city and had left me with oceans of time in which to be not only punctual for school but even to be early.

Me; of a morning; early.

It is known to my friends and family and colleagues that in the earlier parts of a morning you do not find me at my best. Nor, it is to be hoped, do you find me at my worst. The most that can be said, should you have the misfortune to encounter me on my feet quite early any morning, is that I am up.

Why then, all those many years ago, had I wrenched myself from snore, sleepily to shiver under the three brass balls of Uncle, the pawnbroker, and waited to catch the 8.10 a.m. square-wheeled tram?

Who knows what her age may have been, I didn't. Twenty? Eighteen? Twenty-five? All that I had known had been her allure. Her strong, sweet face and her sad, light eyes. Fair hair straightened back, neat and tied into a trim bun. Differently dressed each several day, her proud, large breasts, her dainty waist, the rounded sway of her bottom, the bare slim legs tapering into shoes neat and flat, had had me fair juddering where I stood, bashful and lanky in my short trousers and my shiny black shoes.

Smitten, you might properly think, that gawking, awkward schoolboy which I once had been, baffled by his longing for a woman unknown to him, who perhaps had been twice his age. Feeling for the first disturbing time those anarchic, arbitrary sexual urges which at whiles inhabit us all. Quite right. Nor, for the first few days, had I been able to utter as much as a courteous 'Good morning'. Shufflings I had managed, quite a lot, peerings up the tram tracks to see would this 8.10 a.m. tram ever arrive, checks on the progress of the big hand on Uncle's large clock projecting out over his three brass balls, a keen interest in the objects on display through Uncle's windows, which had allowed me unflustered gazes at the reflected form and features of this lady of my fancy and sometimes, usually from behind but occasionally from almost at her side, barefaced stares at the face and figure of her.

Yes, of course I had wanted her to hug me and hold me to her, but I did so love the arch to her nose, the pout to her mouth and what had seemed to me to be a haughty, weary sadness in her face.

After a while had passed, one day I had been able to muster a proper morning's greeting to her, had been immediately repaid in kind, with the generous addition of a smile, a chuckle and a gaze so steady and so friendly that it had instantly rid her features of their possible sorrow, had rendered me mute, and for the rest of the day my concentration, particularly during school lessons when admittedly it had seldom been at its most intense, had evaporated quite away. Books and pencils and crayons had fallen out of my hands, flights of stairs had been tumbled up, little or less of the sounds or sights of present time had entered my eyes or ears or mind, my very being had been occupied by my darling from the tram stop outside Uncle's and only a violent collision with reality had literally knocked me out of my mooning trance.

After school, head down, trudging through the city, carefully examining the paving stones for no reason in particular, an unbudging lamp-post had reared up suddenly and had fetched me a frightful crack on the nut. Darkness had come to me, followed by a sight of bright stars, the nears and fars, a groggy stagger onto my feet, splitting gyp, and I had wanted my mother and vinegar and brown paper at least.

We shall call my lady Celia and on my morning trots to catch the 8.10 a.m. tram with her, I would try to unknot my tongue by rehearsing to myself lines of the chat that I might have with her: the war, the weather, the price of turnips; matters of pith and moment, for, during the few days of the fewer weeks of this young boy's brief and first encounter with the strong mystery of womanhood, the exchange between us of a few words had meant much to me, and her voice had been clear and gentle. More. On a few of the trips we had actually sat together, upstairs at the back of the swaying and bucking old tram. More. Though Celia had chided me for smoking, and I so young and all, she had produced from her small leather handbag one of the richest and rarest of wartime things: a packet of cigarettes. Pasha. Turkish, allegedly. Previously unknown to me. One for me and one for her and Celia had lit our cigarettes with a lighter fashioned from the brass cartridge of a rifle. More. The lurchings of the tram as it rolled and rattled along the bumping contours of its way had often pushed her to press against me and me against her. At times, Celia had put her arm along the back of the seat, the better for to get a grip against these pitchings and tossings, effectively, though, it had seemed to me, to wrap a loving limb around me. I had used to clutch the front of the seat with both my hands and as every one of the many bends in the tram tracks had approached I had silently beseeched my Maker to give the tramcar an unexpectedly mighty heave and at times my unfathomable Maker had splendidly obliged. Often, for an instant, her head had been thrust against my shoulder, sometimes, alarmingly, our thighs had been squeezed against each other's and, one time, Celia had lost her grip on the seat, had instead grabbed me, had hauled me against her, and for an amazing tick and a tock she had held my head in concert with her jolting breasts.

Celia had chuckled her chuckles and I had whooped my whoops but every raw and young receptor in my eleven-year-old frame had so fizzed and crackled with such rushes of explicit but novel information, that from my toenails to the hairs of my head all had been a vivid and a wonderful shock. Ordinarily it had been her practice to stay on the tram after I had jumped off at the city centre but on one particular morning Celia had stepped off the tram with me at my usual stop. Taller than me by an inch or so, my lady of the tram stop outside Uncle's had looked at me for a second, kissed me lightly on the brow, said, 'Bye bye, Peter, I do wish you well.' She had then turned away from me, glanced both ways, crossed the road, not looked back, turned the corner and had gone. I never saw her again.

After a rueful while, my travels on the 8.20 a.m. tram had been resumed, occasionally lapsing onto the 8.40 but often have I thought of our startling mornings on the 8.10 and my hope is that I always will.

YES, gracious lady, certainly, running all the way. Give me leave awhile to step into these here volumes of flapping great ding dong bell-bottoms, this tarpaulin jacket, and my old hat. Ready; steady; go. Rattling down the line to you, ma'am, able-bodied and in your service. Now, shall I heave from out the Yellow Sea, top-gallant aboard a motor torpedo boat, rip across the Thirty-eighth parallel, stay not near Panmunjom on our starboard bow but wrench her hard to port and skip along the Inchon River to beat backward home these Koreans, these Chinese?

Is it really, ma'am? This news is choice and altogether more sensible these present arrangements. 'Continue our efforts to seek and defend peace.' Assure General Clark, please, that whatever he means he speaks for us all.

Now, with no Korean war to stay me, shall I just offload my dittie box, my steaming bag, my seaboots and my mick? Take, perhaps, a turn around the docks, a cup of tea and a lie down at Sweating Betty's, sell my ring for a tot of neaters, get tattooed, a nap hand, filled in; lose my paybook, crash my swede at the Church of Turkey, muster before the jossman, and then hop on the rattler to swing back up the line all the way home?

Fishes, ma'am? Really? Protect them? Why, yes, of course, ma'am. The protection of the codfish is an altogether admirable undertaking, no less than is the protection of the men who fish for them, the boats in which they trawl and the territorial waters in which they all do swim or sail or hunt it's just that right at this moment I am sweating on the result of a half chance I have of being awarded a scholarship to the Royal Academy of Dramatic Art and, alas, lack an unreserved enthusiasm for slurping about the dip aboard a Fishery Protection Vessel in whatever part of the world it is where you keep your territorial waters.

Iceland, ma'am? Really. That could be at best brisk even in these summer months. Ah well!

197

Balaclava'd, gloved, oilskinned, seabooted, all under my old hat, wet and cold as a witch's tit, bouncing about on a corvette, tied to a flag locker, vomiting in a bucket, typing a weather report. So crucifyingly bored with the raving ache of seasickness that flinging myself into the wash seems at times to me a way of getting it over with, and so a mercy.

The weather blows a bastard and at no time during my days as an active participant in the Cod War do I see so much as another friendly boat leave alone an enemy, nor do I see a fish. Black water galore I see, black rum I drink galore, always we rise and pitch and roll, sometimes I move, sometimes I am flung, at times talk, at whiles sleep in a hammock, mostly I vomit.

When our grim business among the fishes of Icelandic waters had been done, the relief of tottering ashore again in England had been immeasurable. To realise that the street will neither lurch nor heave nor need I brace my legs against the pitching sway, that the winds, the waters, the weather, the seasickness were far far away, had stuck a chuckle on my seafaring gob. This chuckle had resolved itself into whoop of pure delight after I had opened and read a telegram from my father and mother telling me that I had indeed been awarded a scholarship to the RADA. Fees and books and kit for two years all taken care of, a generous chunk of cash each term for shelter, food and clothes, the life of being a student in London and getting paid for it on offer, and an arcane, whimsical instinct within me encouraged to shape up to this business of becoming an actor.

Well, really, I had been elected.

At the Arms Park in Cardiff, Jim the Pill, Sid the Id, the untouchable Griffith and I, all there to see the rugger, I said to Sid, 'When does childhood end?' and Sid said, 'Oh, pre-puberty, ten or eleven, that's about the size of it.'

Yes, Sid, that had been about the size of it.